Bernice Rubens was born in Cardiff and is a graduate of Cardiff University. After graduating she became an actress but left the stage for teaching. In 1970 Bernice Rubens won the Booker Prize for Fiction, Britain's most important literary award, for her fourth novel, *The Elected Member*. Her ninth novel, *A Five Year Sentence*, was short-listed for the Booker Prize in 1978 and she is the author of many literary works including, *Go Tell the Lemming*, *I Sent a Letter to my Love*, *The Ponsonby Post*, *Sunday Best*, *Mate in Three* and *Set on Edge*.

The Elected Member

BERNICE RUBENS

SPHERE BOOKS LIMITED
30–32 Gray's Inn Road, London WC1X 8JL

First published by Eyre & Spottiswoode 1969
Copyright © Bernice Rubens 1969
Published by Sphere Books Ltd 1980

**TRADE
MARK**

Set in Intertype Times

Set, printed and bound in Great Britain by
Cox & Wyman Ltd, Reading

for Rudi

If patients are *disturbed*, their families are often very *disturbing*.

R. D. LAING
The Politics of Experience

1

Norman Zweck dared not open his eyes. He turned over on his stomach, raised his knee high, stiffening straight the other leg. He slipped his toe into the division of the two mattresses, savouring the chill of the other side, the inherited side. Once it had been his parents' bed, a vast seven-footer, mahogany-joined at both ends for form's sake, but divided in the middle for all practical purposes. Together but divided they had lain for forty-five years of their marriage. When his mother had died, two years before, she had, on that very bed, but on the other side, bequeathed it to him. His father had gladly taken over his son's single bedroom, while Norman lay chained to his inheritance. Occasionally, he had slipped over to his cold legacy during his fitful sleeps. But nightmares awaited him on that side, and terrible wakenings. He edged over for safety to his father's side, stiffening again his one leg, and embedding his other foot into the dividing line, and without touching his body, he felt the feel of it. A young boy, he thought, would have felt the same sensation in the youthful stretch of the leg, and the relaxed hollow between the shoulder blades. So he did not touch the folds on his stomach, or the veined stretches of his groin. These were intellectualized realities, and had nothing to do with the teenage lay-out of his body. He slipped his hand underneath the pillow, grazing his stubbled cheek. He smiled sadly at this undeniable touch of age, and to confirm it, grasped with his calloused hands, the wrinkled folds of his flesh. He gathered them up, one by one the muscle-less wads on his belly, his chin and his thighs, twisting and turning them, obsessed by their feel of years. He returned to his original lay-out, but now he knew it for a fraud. The folds and wrinkles on his skin, were notches, each one, for each of his forty-one years.

He screwed his eyes tightly against the dark. He knew that his short sleep was over, but he was too terrified to acknowledge it. He should never have let himself doze off. God knows what they were doing while he was sleeping, and God knows what they were doing now, and where else they were, and how many. No, he would not open his eyes. If they were still there, he could rely on them to stay. He pulled the pillow over his ears. He didn't want to hear them either. Yet he wanted to check that they were still there. He dreaded their presence, but their sudden absence would have terrified him more. They were the only witnesses to his sanity.

He opened his eyes, first to the darkness under the pillow, and then to the darkness in the room, and it frightened him. He got up and groped for the light, and squinting, quickly returned to his blanket cocoon. Slowly, he adjusted his eyes to the light, and he lay there, staring at his legacy on the other side. He felt a stinging behind his eyes as a prelude to tears and it surprised him. He had plenty to cry about, but he had never given in to any feeling of self-pity. Quite often, he had thought to put an end to it all, but he had to convince somebody, at least one person before he went, otherwise, in their eyes, he would die a madman. But nobody would listen to him any more. Nobody believed him. Nobody had the willingness or the patience to sit with him for a while, if necessary for hours, and see them like he saw them, and catch a little of his fear.

He stroked the virgin sheet alongside him, over and over again. And suddenly on the skin of his palm, he felt the grazing of a curve and a line. As he lowered his hand, he uncovered, as in a brass rubbing, the head, shoulders and prone body of his mother. His hand lay paralysed where her legs would lie, and terrified, he clawed down the sheet and revealed her entire. As he stared at her, he felt ice-cold tears blotting the fire on his cheeks. He opened his mouth to call her, but refrained. He didn't want to acknowledge her presence. He told himself it was a nightmare. But perhaps the other things were nightmares too, perhaps there was nothing in the room, save his own tormented soul in its worn and wrinkled packaging. Perhaps it was all a hallucination. 'No,' he screamed into the sheets. Not that word. Not that filthy rotten family word, that his father and his sister had picked up from his psychiatrist. They were blind, all of

8

them, and they tossed the word at each other knowingly yet shamefully, comforted by its overtones of impermanence. 'He's hallucinating,' they would nod at each other, and he could have killed them for their cosiness.

He stared at his mother again. She was there, sure enough, and so were all the other things. *She* would have seen them. *She* would have acknowledged them and got rid of them. She would have delivered him. 'Mama,' he whispered, but the curve and line dissolved into the sheet. Even *he* saw that she was gone, and over the years he had become an expert in the appearance and disappearance of things. But he knew she would come again, and he lay in wait for her, his cold hand spread over the sheet.

He lifted his ear from the pillow and he heard them, the scratching teeth-gnashing grind of their crawl. And something new too. Their smell. At first, he held his breath, then he sniffed gratefully around him. A dewy smell, like biscuits left un-covered, to soften. It was further proof that they were there. They had a right after all, to make a noise and to emanate some kind of odour. But he was frightened too. Each further proof of their presence frightened him. The more overwhelming the evi-dence, the less credulous his family became. He buried his head in the pillow, clasping his body with his hands. Slowly his fingers moved, scratching along the flesh of his shoulders. He tried to ignore what his fingers were doing, and he began hum-ming a tune to give his fingers some excuse for drumming on his back. But his fingers ignored the rhythm, scratching in spas-modic frenzy all over his body. He started to sing loudly, but his fingers refused to accompany him. Then, beaten, he buried his head in the pillow, and acknowledged that they were on him. They were crawling on his back, sponging the sweat that trickled down his spine, loitering on his hip-bone, and sliding slimy into his groin. He leapt out of bed, grabbing the pillow, and ran through the darkness into the bathroom. He threw the pillow into the bath and dowsed it with boiling water. He knew they were in the pillow, alive and therefore killable. He took a bottle of Dettol from the cupboard and slopped it over his body. He would entertain them as long as they were on the floor and window-sills, but on his body, never. He had to teach them to know their place. That much he had to control. Why then, he wondered, could he not wipe them clean from the floor as he intended to do from his body. Perhaps they didn't exist at all, anywhere. He caught the shadow of his face in the mirror above the sink. He did not recognize the image that stared back at him, and he clenched his fist at it, and screamed, 'Are you going mad?' and sobbing he shuffled back to his room to greet them.

He turned off his light, and avoiding the bed, groped his way to their accustomed hang-out around the fireplace. He reached for his torch on the mantelpiece and shone it obliquely towards one corner of the room. As he waited he scratched himself with his free hand. He hoped that the bites and their scars were visible. It would be undeniable proof to his father. The smell was overpowering, but he wallowed in it. That too, was proof. His father would come in the morning to waken him, and he would have to notice it. Until then, he would sit and watch them, and try to overcome his fear.

They did not keep him waiting long, because he was more than ready for them. They crawled in single file towards the beam of light, and in its pool, they stopped, congregated and wriggled. A swarm of twisting silver-fish, as he had seen them every day and night that he could remember, for the days and nights he had forgotten had been erased by his madness. He shifted the beam of the torch over to his right, teasing the insects to another halt. In such a manner, Norman Zweck perambulated his flock around the fireplace through the lightening dark, that soon cancelled out the torch. Then suddenly they disappeared. Norman curled himself up by the fire-place, staring, sniffing and scratching, hanging on the smell of them and the feel of them, and searching for their traces along the worn rug by the fire. He always dreaded this hour of the day, when the light drove them into obscurity and he was left with only the memory of their creeping promenade. It was now that fear invaded him fully, and the dread question that he had managed to hurl at the man in the bathroom mirror. He watched the globules of sweat as they grew full and exploded on his arms and legs. He indulged in his fear as it melted his bowel, saun-tered over his thighs, and lodged in the bed of his knees. 'They're here,' he whispered to himself, 'I see them, I smell them, I scratch them on my flesh.' He clutched his body into his arms, embracing his despair. Then with the conviction that only a lunatic can achieve, he shrieked aloud, 'I know they are here.'

He crawled on to the foot of the bed, rubbing his itching flesh against the raw blanket. When morning came, he was asleep, and had his father known of his son's night, he would not have woken him.

2

But at eight o'clock, as was his custom, Rabbi Zweck came into Norman's room to wake him. He hesitated as he saw him crumpled at the foot of the bed, but he did not allow the position to unnerve him. His son had had a restless night, a bad dream maybe; everybody did from time to time. Even when the smell of Dettol hit him, he tried to dismiss its known associations. He tapped his son gently on the shoulder. 'Norman,' he said, 'is eight o'clock.'

Norman responded immediately, and as he raised his head, he saw his father sniffing around the room. He jumped off the bed, wild with gratitude. 'You can smell them?' he said.

Rabbi Zweck turned pale. It was starting all over again. This was the fifth breakdown in less than a year. 'Dettol, I smell,' he shouted angrily. 'That's what I smell. Dettol.' His anxiety exploded inside him with automatic anger at the mad. 'Nothing to smell,' he screamed at him again, 'only Dettol. Get up, *meshuggana*. Breakfast is ready.'

Rabbi Zweck slammed the door. He doubted whether he could survive if Norman collapsed again. He heard the key turn in his son's door and the sound sickened him. As he stood outside the kitchen, he shuddered at his own loneliness, but the sense of his son's isolation behind the locked door, almost killed him.

Norman waited for his father's slippered tread to die away. Then he got down on his knees, and scrambled at a loose floorboard underneath the bed for his day's supply. Wedged under the board was an old cardigan, and from its wrapping he extracted a large bottle. He held it up and looked at its level. He was frightened that it was so low. He had bought the bottle only a week ago, and he panicked at the thought of getting money for more. He poured a handful into his palm, remembering the old days, years ago it seemed, when he'd tentatively taken just one. He stuffed them into his mouth hurriedly screwing on the cap at the same time. He replaced the floorboards, and got shakily to his feet, Then quietly he unlocked his door and opened it. He heard the whisperings of his father and sister in the kitchen. They thought he was mad. Oh not that. That couldn't happen in their family. He was just being perverse. He was breaking their hearts for want of something better to do. It was not his agony. It was theirs. 'Silver-fish,' he heard his father muttering, 'again with his silver-fish. Whoever heard of fish crawling on a carpet? Water they need. But no. My son's fish, such a clever son I have, on carpets they can live, in pillows, in sheets. Insects, he calls them. Fish are fish,' he yelled at his daughter as if she were denying it. 'On the carpet they should be. Huh.'

'Shut the door, for heaven's sake,' he heard Bella whisper, and he knew that they had begun to conspire against him. He did not bother to wash or dress. He wanted to interrupt their plotting. He threw on a dressing-gown, and tip-toed to the kitchen. Then suddenly he burst open the door. His sister stopped mid-sentence, and began to fuss over his place at the table. As he came over to sit down, she started sniffing at him.

'Can you smell something?' he asked with waning optimism.

'Dettol she smells,' his father jumped in to answer for her.

'They're all over the place,' he threatened them. 'They're on my body too. You must be a couple of blind insensitive bastards if you can't see them.' Although vulgarity always accompanied Norman's hallucinations, Rabbi Zweck could never get used to it. In the rare intervals of his son's sanity, and the accompanying good relations between them both, he forgot the crudity, he forgot the belligerence, and when they appeared, it was always as if for the first time. He looked across at his son, forcing himself to remember the boy's innate gentleness. It was not his son who was rambling on about his silver-fish; it was some devil that possessed him, some evil eye in temporary lodging. And when he saw his son as one possessed, Rabbi Zweck found it easier to forgive him. He stretched out his hand over the table and covered his son's with his own.

Norman snatched his hand away. 'I'm going to ring up the Health Authorities.'

'Again?' Bella said wearily. 'They came,' she tried to be patient with him, 'they came two months ago. They went through the house with a tooth-comb. They took away samples you gave them. They tested them in laboratories. All they found was carpet fluff and dirt. You had their letter. In black and white. What more d'you want?'

'They were here for five minutes,' Norman shouted at her, 'What did they expect to find in five minutes? They've got to pull up the carpets and do it thoroughly. Don't you bloody well *care*,' he shouted at them, 'that you've got them crawling all over the place?'

'Eat your breakfast,' his father said gently.

Norman tapped his father's arm and grinned at him. 'I bet you've got them all over your body too.'

It was the grin that finished Rabbi Zweck. During his son's breakdown, he often had the feeling that Norman was having him on. That he was just driving him mad for the kick of it. 'You think you are so funny,' he shouted at him, and he slapped Norman's cheek with the back of his ringed hand.

'You'll be sorry for that,' Norman said quietly.

Nobody said anything for a long time. Norman rubbed his stubbled cheek, and Bella watched her father choking back his tears. Once or twice, she saw him open his mouth to speak, but his voice was not yet ready. She heard him mutter an apology. Then he tried again.

'Norman,' he said gently. He hesitated, fearful of what he knew he must ask. 'Norman,' he said again, 'where d'you get them from? How many have you taken?'

'I haven't got any,' Norman shouted. 'I haven't taken any. I haven't taken any for years.'

Rabbi Zweck lost his temper again. 'Who is the murderer who gives them to you? I'll kill him. I'll kill him,' he was crying with the agony of it. 'What for you want to take them?' he begged. 'Stop it with the pills already or I shall go mad.'

'Why d'you have to do it to him?' Bella shouted. 'Can't you see it's killing him? What are you trying to do to us?'

14

Rabbi Zweck buried his head in his hands. 'Stop it with the bloody pills already,' he said feebly. He hated his own unfamiliar language, but he had used it deliberately as a desperate bid for his son's confidence. 'I'll ring Dr Levy,' he said, getting up.

'You keep that bastard out of this house,' Norman said. 'I'm not having him here. What's he know about anything, that tit. You bring him here, and I'll kill him.' He pushed his unfinished breakfast away from him, and strode out of the room. They waited, listening, until they heard his key turn in the door.

'Poor, poor boy,' Rabbi Zweck muttered, and he went to the telephone.

'Dr Levy?'

'Rabbi Zweck,' the doctor said. He recognized the voice and he knew what it wanted. The calls were getting more frequent.

'It's silver-fish again,' the Rabbi said, and he hated the contempt for his son that he heard in his own voice.

'I'll come right away.'

Rabbi Zweck put down the phone. He was shivering with his son's fear. He wished to God he could see them like his son saw them, that they could go into madness together, hand in hand. It was his son's loneliness that stabbed him like a knife, his yellow-faced boy, haggard with the terror of his imaginings, no doubt at this moment sitting crouched on his infested floor, trapping his evidence. 'I'll tell him I can see them,' the Rabbi said to himself. 'Perhaps he'll stop the joke already.'

He tapped on Norman's door. 'Norman,' he called.

'What d'you want?'

'Norman,' he repeated softly. 'They still there? I should have another look?'

There was a silent suspicion behind the door.

'I should have another look?' Rabbi Zweck pleaded.

The key turned in the lock and the door opened gingerly. It was dark in the room. The curtains were drawn, and books held them down at each corner to block out the light.

'You've got to be very quiet,' Norman whispered.

His father watched his son's drawn face and the black eyes that swelled out of it. The dark and the whisperings made him ashamed and he wondered what God must think of his behaviour. He hoped He wasn't misled by it. Who was He punishing anyway, he thought, himself, or his son.

'Stand by the fire-place,' Norman was saying. 'Be quiet. You'll see plenty, if you just wait.'

But Rabbi Zweck was prepared to see without waiting. 'I can see them,' he whispered, staring at the empty carpet. He raised himself on his toes, excitedly. 'My, my,' he marvelled, 'so many, like an army they are.' He looked at his son for his gratitude.

'You think I'm mad, don't you?' Norman said quietly. 'Look here,' he opened a drawer. Inside, wedged in the corner, was a glass jar, with a few leaves that rested on red carpet fluff on the bottom. Opposite the jar was a magnifying mirror. 'Look in that mirror,' Norman said, 'you'll see them all right.'

'Leaves I see,' Rabbi Zweck said bewildered.

'I'm feeding them,' Norman laughed.

He wanted to hit his son again, but instead, he left the room quietly.

'Don't come back,' Norman almost sobbed at him. 'Leave me alone. Just leave me alone.'

The key turned in the door, and Rabbi Zweck went back to the kitchen. 'Go down, open the shop,' he said. 'Is already nine o'clock.'

As she passed him, Bella put her hand on his shoulder. 'Don't worry,' she said, 'he'll be over it soon.'

'And then again it starts.' He clutched at her arm. 'We must find them,' he said desperately. 'We must get him out of that room and you must find them. They're there. He's getting them from someone. If ever I lay my hands on him, I'll. ... You haven't done the room thoroughly enough,' he shouted at her. He bit his lip to stem the tears. 'Go, go,' he said quickly, 'open the shop. On top of everything I should lose the business too.'

He caught sight of her white ankle-socks as she left the room. She was forty, almost, his Bella, and still in her girlhood socks. But that was another agony. He daren't give any thought to that one. He sniffed his tears away and waited for the doctor.

When the bell rang, he heard Norman shout, 'If that's that shit Levy, tell him to piss off.'

16

Rabbi Zweck knew that Dr Levy must have heard through the door and he began apologizing on his son's behalf as he let the doctor in.

'Don't worry,' Dr Levy said, 'it's natural. Can we go into the kitchen?' he whispered. He knew Norman would be listening by his door, and he didn't want to be overheard. He followed Rabbi Zweck into the kitchen and sat at the table. He had become familiar with the room. The copper ladle that hung over the kitchen sink was always at the same angle and with the same high polish. In the cup of lemon tea that Rabbi Zweck put before him, he saw the familiar and now fading rose pattern that lined the cup. He was not their official family doctor. Dr Levy was a psychiatrist, but he was a long-standing friend of the Zweck family. As a friend, he had been in on Mrs Zweck's dying, sitting on the same chair by the kitchen table, drinking tea out of a less faded rose-patterned cup. Then he had sat with Rabbi Zweck much as he was doing now, comforting him, the truth exposed between them. 'It's only a matter of time,' he had told the Rabbi then, 'and the sooner, the better for you all.' Meanwhile, in the vast seven-footer, Mrs Zweck wondered why she was taking so long to recover from her operation. 'It takes longer when you're older,' the doctor had told her. 'Another month or so and you'll be up and about.' So she lay there, having patience, fingering the holiday brochure that Rabbi Zweck had bought her, to help her decide where to convalesce. Now, it was Norman, on the same bed, with a different illusion, but an illusion all the same, while between his father and Dr Levy in the kitchen, straddled the same uneasy truth.

'How long has he been like this?' Dr Levy asked.

'How should I know,' Rabbi Zweck said helplessly. 'For many days now he doesn't eat. Breakfast he has, a big breakfast, and afterwards, nothing.'

'Has he been in the shop?'

'He goes downstairs. He sits. He does nothing, Bella says. And always so rude, I'm ashamed for my customers. If only I knew where he got them. If only . . .'

'Rabbi Zweck,' the doctor said gently, 'even if you found where he was getting them, it would be of no use. He'd find

17

another source. They're all the same, these addicts. They're so cunning. Come what may, they'll find somewhere to get it. It's expensive of course. Does he have so much money?'

Rabbi Zweck was silent. Then without looking at Doctor Levy, he stretched his hand towards him over the table. 'Doctor,' he said, 'I'm ashamed, but you're a doctor, and is confidence what I tell you.' Dr Levy patted the Rabbi's hand.

'He's stealing it?' he said.

Rabbi Zweck hung his head. 'My own son,' he whispered, 'a *ganuf*, and from his father's money. The till,' he said, 'last week, my Bella is missing fifteen pounds. What can I do? Every minute I can't be with him.' Dr Levy opened his black case. 'We must get him better, at least over this bout, then we must try again to persuade him to go to hospital. It's the only way. Six months, a year, away from the drug. He might get over it.'

'I've tried,' the Rabbi said, 'Bella's tried. Each time he gets over it, he says he'll stop it. Then he starts again. What will become of him?'

'Let's get him over this lot first,' the doctor said business-like.

Rabbi Zweck squeezed the doctor's hand. 'I am thinking,' he said, 'perhaps *takka* is silver-fish in his room. Perhaps when they come from the cleaning people, they don't look so thoroughly. Like Norman said, a real spring-clean we should have. So we should find them and take them away.' He looked at Dr Levy pleadingly.

'You will drive yourself mad,' Dr Levy whispered. 'You are trying to defend him at the risk of your own sanity. There is nothing in his room. You know it as well as I. Listen Rabbi, it's very simple.' Dr Levy leaned forward and spoke very slowly with the patience of one who has explained the same situation over and over again. 'When he started to take the drugs, they gave him what they call, a kick. You understand?'

'What should I know from a kick,' Rabbi Zweck said wearily. At each of Norman's breakdowns and at each ex-planation, he refused to acknowledge that the diagnosis had anything to do with his son. 'Doctors' talk,' he muttered to himself. 'A real spring-clean Bella will give,' he said.

'When Norman started,' Dr Levy went on, ignoring the interruption, 'it took just one tablet to make him feel good. Then as time went on, in order to get the same effect, he had to take more, and more and more. Until, like now, he's taking them by the handful. Now these drugs are dangerous. If you take enough of them, you begin to see things, things that other people don't see. Snakes, elephants, pins, or like Norman, silver-fish. He sees them all right, but he's hallucinating. They're not there, Rabbi Zweck,' Dr Levy said firmly, 'no matter how much he convinces you. You know they're not there, don't you.'

Rabbi Zweck sighed. Sometimes he hated Dr Levy. 'How are you so sure they're not there?' he mumbled.

Dr Levy took a small tablet out of the box. 'I won't go in and see him,' he said. 'It will only make him worse. Persuade him to join you and Bella for some coffee during the morning, and crush this into the sugar. Let Bella do it. It will dissolve and with luck he won't taste it. If he drinks the whole cup, he'll sleep for a few hours and I'll come over later and give him an injection. Same as before. We'll give him deep sedation for a fortnight. Like last time.'

'And the time before that,' the Rabbi put in. 'And the next time.'

'Let's cross this hurdle, shall we, and afterwards we'll try to talk to him. All of us. It's you I'm worried about, Rabbi. More than Norman,' Dr Levy said. 'You're letting it kill you.'

'You want I should dance?' Rabbi Zweck muttered.

'Remember the times when he's all right. In between the bouts. These times are time to live for and look forward to. The times when he's a good son to you.'

'They're not so often, these times. Not any more,' Rabbi Zweck said. He banged his fist on the table in sudden anger. 'I should only find the murderer who sells them to him.'

'Walk me downstairs to the shop,' the doctor said gently. 'You can sell me some cigarettes.'

Rabbi Zweck stopped at his son's door. 'Norman,' he called.

'You can tell Dr Levy from me,' Norman shouted, 'he's a psychiatrist like the cat's a psychiatrist, and he can take his injections to hell. There's nothing the matter with me,' he yelled,

19

half-sobbing. 'It's you and your lot. You're mad, the lot of you. Just leave me alone.'

'I'm going downstairs to the shop,' his father said evenly. 'Soon I'll come back. We'll have a tea together, huh. You, me and Bella.'

'I don't want any family conferences,' Norman said. 'Just leave me alone.'

Dr Levy put his arm round Rabbi Zweck's shoulder and led him downstairs to the shop.

An hour later Bella and her father left the shop in charge of the assistant and returned to the flat. They whispered together in the kitchen as Bella ground the white pill into the sugar at the bottom of the glass. Then she covered the mixture with a piece of lemon.

'It'll be better once he's sleeping, Poppa. We'll have to ask Auntie Sadie to come over again and look after him. Shall I phone her?'

'This is already the sixth time.'

'She loves it. You know she does. I'll phone her from downstairs.'

'Wait. Wait till he sleeps,' her father said. 'Then we'll see.'

The tea was ready and they stared at each other, neither of them willing to call Norman.

'You should tell him his tea's ready,' Rabbi Zweck said.

'You tell him. He won't listen to me. All right,' she said, seeing him hesitate, 'I'll tell him.'

She shouted through the passage, 'Norman, your tea's ready.'

'Norman, your tea's ready,' he mimicked her.

'You want your tea or don't you?' she said angrily.

'You want your tea or don't you,' came from behind the door.

Bella went back to the kitchen. 'I can't get anywhere with him,' she said. Rabbi Zweck got up wearily and went down the corridor. 'Norman,' he called gently. 'You want tea?'

'I told you. I don't want a family conference. You'll have Auntie Sadie here next in a white coat pulling a Florence Nightingale on me.'

'You want it in your room?' his father said timidly.

'Put it outside the door.'

'Please,' Bella prompted from the kitchen. She found it hard to treat him as an invalid. She wanted to punish him for what he was doing to her father. To her too, for he had already done enough to her. She looked down at her feet. Of course, she didn't have to go on wearing those white ankle-socks. But it was habit by now. She would have to start being another person if she wore anything else. That was all his fault too. She resented the feeling of obligation she felt for him. They had nothing in common; all they shared were the same parents, the same miserable childhood, and the same mutual embarrassment. She tried not to wish him dead.

Rabbi Zweck picked up Norman's cup from the table. 'This one?' he said. He gave it an extra stir and carried it to his son's door. 'It's outside, Norman,' he said. 'Careful, is hot.'

He returned to the kitchen where they both sat and waited. They heard Norman's door open and close again. Rabbi Zweck peeped out and saw that the cup had gone. 'Thank God,' he said, 'at least he'll drink it.' But hardly had Rabbi Zweck sat down again than they heard Norman open his door. 'What d'you think I am?' he was yelling. 'D'you think I can't taste it?' He stormed into the kitchen, and put the cup on the table. 'What are you trying to do? Murder me?'

'What, what?' Rabbi Zweck mumbled, 'what's the matter?'

'You've put something in my tea,' Norman said. 'Go on, taste it.'

'There's nothing in your tea,' Bella said coldly. 'We've all got the same. It all came out of the same pot.'

'Is the lemon perhaps too bitter?' Rabbi Zweck tried. Deception was not his forte.

'Lemon, my arse,' Norman said. 'Go on then, if you're so sure there's nothing in it, *you* drink it.' He pushed the cup towards his father.

Rabbi Zweck had not envisaged this eventuality. But he had no alternative. He picked up the cup gingerly and took as small a sip as was possible without raising his son's suspicions. 'Is all right,' he said. 'Perhaps more sugar you need.'

'Drink some more,' Norman ordered, 'you'll taste it.'

The Rabbi raised his cup again to his lips, while Norman stood over him measuring his dose. 'More, more,' he kept saying, until his father had drained half the cup.

'Is all right,' he said again.

'You taste it then,' Norman pushed the cup over to Bella.

Bella was horrified to discover how much her father had drunk.

'Go on,' Norman said, as he saw her hesitate, 'Poison yourself a little.'

She took a mouthful. It had an undeniably bitter taste. Dr Levy must have been crazy to think that Norman, with his gourmet taste in drugs, would not have noticed it. She hated Dr Levy. She hated everybody for all they'd done to her. She hated her sister Esther for marrying and opting out of the responsibility. She hated Norman for what he was doing to all of them, and even her father because of the love she could not deny him. 'There's nothing wrong with it,' she said, 'it's your imagination. Like your silver-fish.'

She hated herself for saying it. Why couldn't she pretend her brother had jaundice, or measles, or rheumatism, or any other respectable talkable-of malady. She looked at the black stubble that shadowed his jaw and the sallow shadings on his cheeks. He looked ill, terribly ill. Wasn't that enough for her?

Norman pushed the cup back to his father. 'Go on, taste it,' he said petulantly, 'you know there's something in it.'

Rabbi Zweck took another dutiful mouthful, and pronounced his verdict. 'Nothing,' he said. He already felt drowsy and he put his hand to his forehead.

'Leave him alone, can't you,' Bella said.

'Well, you taste it again then,' he sulked. 'If anyone's going to croak in this house, it's not going to be me.' He stood over her while she drank. After a mouthful, Bella managed to put the cup down.

'Well,' he said, standing at the door, 'I wish you long life, both of you.' Bella heard him stamp back to his room and lock the door behind him.

'What now?' she said helplessly. Her father slipped his head over the table. She shook him gently, but he was fast asleep. She sat beside him wondering how to shoulder the responsibility alone. She couldn't forget the look on her brother's face as he stood over her watching her drink. If only she had not been his sister, she could have put her arm round him and believed in him for his sake. She could even have loved him. But blood was a buffer to that kind of loving, the unselfish kind. She had loved him once and he, her, when they were both children and she legitimately in those white socks. Neither had mentioned it since, no one had ever shared their secret, though God knows, the thought occurred to her, Dr Levy must have got it out of him by now. She got up to clear the table, but felt her knees give way beneath her. She didn't try to fight it, she wanted to opt out of it all for a while. She even hoped she'd sleep for ever. She slumped back on to her chair and surrendered to the stupor that gradually overcame her.

Norman pushed the sideboard against the door and squatted on the floor. Even though he had drawn his curtains, the light that insisted through the thin material, had driven his companions away. He decided he would buy some thick velvet curtains, lined with heavy black, so that it would be night in his room always with his crawling proof around him. It was in the daylight and in his undeniable lack of company, that the terrifying question of his sanity nagged at him. Even to ask it of himself was an admission that his father and sister had a case to argue. No, he must not on any account allow that question, but with what force, in the naked daylight, could he oust it from him? He sat there, unarmed, the question surrounding him. It was only a matter of time before it would gently invade his privacy. Am I mad? Are there really silver-fish? If there are, where are they now? It's Bella's fault that she's given me these curtains. They scurry away from the light. Why did she not believe him? Nor his father? What particular madness did they have that they were so blind to his sanity? And if they couldn't see them, why should it then outrage *him*? Now the questions had had their fill and were satisfied, and they left him wounded and alone, waiting through the long day for the night to come and gather his forces.

He heard the door bell ring. They were coming to fetch him. It was that clot Levy with his needle coming to put him to sleep, like last time. He leapt up and moved the chest of drawers against the door. He only wanted to hold out till nightfall, when more evidence would be available. Then he would let them in, all of them. 'Then we'll see who's mad,' he said to himself. He listened, but no one seemed to be answering the door. He hadn't heard anyone go out, so his father and sister must still be in the flat. He hoped that the caller, whoever it was, would go away, but the bell rang again, longer this time, and repeatedly. He waited. In between rings, he heard the silence in the flat. They had slipped out without his hearing. Where had they gone? Had they gone to fetch someone to take him away? And was that someone already at the door? He heard the letter-box flap. 'Miss Zweck?' a high-pitched voice hissed through the hall. It was Terry, the assistant in the shop. He was safe, little too, and frail. Norman moved the sideboard away and opened his door. 'What d'you want?' he called through the hall. 'Miss Zweck,' Terry said. 'She hasn't come back to the shop. It's my lunch hour.'

'She's not here,' Norman said. 'You'll have to go downstairs and wait for her. Sorry,' he added. He felt very tender towards the boy, as the only person in his orbit who did not think he was mad. Terry had seen them. One night after the shop had closed, and his father and sister were out, Terry had come to his room and seen them. He had stood riveted to the carpet, terrified, his hand clutching the door to run away from them. 'I can't stand it,' he said eventually. Norman let him go, grateful for his understanding.

'Can't *you* come down?' Terry said timidly.

'I can't. I'm trying to get rid of the things in my room.'

He heard Terry's steps down the stone stairway, taking them two by two, and landing on the stone floor at the foot of the stairs.

Norman stood in the empty hall. He wondered where they had gone. He heard a faint breathing noise, and with overwhelming joy, he knew they had come back to his room. But the noise grew faint as he entered. Then he heard it behind him, echoing through the hall. He leaned against his door, taking in the full meaning of this new development. Without doubt they were in there, in complete and total invasion of the whole flat,

24

He was satisfied. Now they would *have* to listen to him, because they were everywhere. He was vindicated. But he wouldn't revenge himself on them. He would be gentle and tolerant, and forgive them their accusations. He longed for his father and sister to come back. He opened his bedroom door wide, and drew his curtains. He no longer needed his privacy. He walked through the hall towards the kitchen. He noticed how the noise increased, but it did not trouble him. The kitchen was the obvious place for them to congregate in a mass. He himself had seen them there before; in fact, there were few places he didn't see them, if he wished to look. But now they had grown tired of being ignored, and they had come to the kitchen in armies, for recognition. He reached the kitchen door. It was ajar and the noise by now was thunderous. He hesitated with joy, postponing the final confirmation of what he knew would be his salvation. Then he threw the door open wide.

His father sat there, slumped over the table. Snoring. His father was snoring. That was all. Even Norman, to whom sounds of life and death and the imagination had become so confused, even he had to equate the noise with his sleeping father. Bella, at his side, contributed a humble descant to her father's theme. What an ugly pair they are, he thought. He looked at Bella's white socked feet under the table, and the coarse tufts of black hair that the elastic had bunched around the rim. Everyone blamed him for those socks, but Christ, she didn't have to go on wearing them. He avoided looking at her face. He had loved her once, because it was forbidden. Really, he reflected, the only time in his life he had loved. He looked quickly at his father. His skull cap had slipped over on to one ear, and the visible half of his head was veined like an old woman's hand. This was the man who had told him that the sea had parted for the Jews, the man who believed in miracles, the man who believed in all good men except his own son. Norman felt pity for him, but he stood his ground. He would not allow himself to be moved, neither by his father's old head nor his sister's white socks. He had to go on hating them, until they would begin to understand. He took his stand between the two of them, and opening his mouth, he let out a long piercing scream. They moved simultaneously, the one towards the other, as if in half-sleep, sensing disaster, and seeking protection. Bella was the first to open her eyes, but she quickly closed them again, as if to obliterate the split-second reality she had faced. Rabbi Zweck opened his eyes slowly, moaned, and kept them open. His sleep had been profound, but it had embraced all the while, the picture of his son's tragedy. So he looked at Norman and adjusted quickly, because not for a second in his sleep had he dismissed him. Bella opened her eyes again and was compelled to come to terms with the awakening. 'The tea,' she said to herself, that he had survived, her mad brother, with his silver-fish. And his sister Esther, married and out of it all, and their mother dead, and him killing their father with his madness. She stood up and put her arm on her father's shoulder. 'What shall we do?' she said helplessly.

'What time is it?' Rabbi Zweck asked.

'It's just two.'

'Then what about Terry's lunch?' he said. He grasped at the problem as something concrete. At least it was a problem that could be solved, and quickly. 'Go, look after the shop,' he said to Bella.

'What about *him*?' Bella said. She gave him the anonymity of a lunatic. 'What are we going to do about him?' Her anger and hatred were consuming her.

'Don't worry about me,' Norman said, 'I'm going to burn up my carpet and get rid of them.' He smiled at her innocently.

'Oh God,' she said, collapsing on to a chair, 'how much more must we take? You're wrong,' she screamed at him suddenly, 'there are no insects in this flat. You're wrong, you're wrong,' she shouted. 'Madmen are always wrong.'

Norman went back to his room. He leaned against the keyhole and listened for the next move. After a while, he heard Bella walking across the hall and out of the door, and the ring on the telephone as his father began to dial. He moved away from the door. His father was calling Dr Levy; they would go through it all again. He became suddenly weary of the whole situation. 'It would be so much easier if I were really mad,' he said to himself. 'Then they would make me better and I wouldn't see them any more.' He toyed with the idea of pretending he was mad, so that they could 'cure' him, and then after the 'cure', he would still see them, and maybe then they would believe him. But he couldn't pretend he was mad. 'Only fringe madmen can fake lunacy,' he said to himself. 'I could never take them in. Why, even that clot Levy would see through me. Straight away. He thinks I'm mad, but only as long as I'm sane. He's got to think that. It's his living. If old Levy ever thought I was sane, I'd *really* get worried.' He smiled to himself. They were all mad, all of them, and with this supreme conviction, he locked his door.

His father was still on the telephone, but he did not want to listen. He didn't want to be forced into making plans. Deep inside him, he felt the terrible pre-pain of surrender, that he had felt a few months ago, when Dr Levy's needle had jabbed his arm. 'This time,' he said aloud, 'I must resist them. I'm right, I'm right,' he screeched into himself, and he heard the echo of his sister's contrary accusation.

He squatted on the floor and tried not to think of what they would do to him. After a time, he heard the letter-box rattle and he waited for his father to open the door.

'Does Norman Zweck live here?' he heard a man's voice say, and somehow or other he knew that the man was carrying documents in his hand.

There were two of them, clad in black and bureaucracy, with identical brown briefcases, and Rabbi Zweck let them in. Like two undertakers, they could well have carried a tape-measure.

'Could we go somewhere and talk,' one of the doctors inquired, looking around the hall for a convenient corner.

'In the kitchen,' Rabbi Zweck said tonelessly, and the two men followed him. They sat down at the table and came to the point straight away. 'Dr Levy has told us the position,' one of them said. 'You understand of course, that it is necessary for us to see your son. We have to recommend that he is suitable for hospital treatment. It's the law, you know,' he added gently.

'Yes, it's the law,' Rabbi Zweck repeated. He could not understand why he had let these two men into the flat. He had invited them in to certify his son. He was helping them to put his boy away. He was agreeing with them that his son was mad. 'But,' he started to protest, realizing the magnitude of the situation, 'is absolute necessary he should go to the hospital? Is only a little mad, my son,' he pleaded. 'I'll tell him he shouldn't take the pills any more, and he'll get better. I promise you,' he was pleading with them. 'I promise you, on my poor wife's memory, *olav hasholem*.' (what did these *goyim* know of such things?) 'He's not mad,' he protested, 'my son. Is tired he is a little. Not much sleep he's had, is confused in his mind a little. I also, when I'm tired, a little bit *zemischt* I am.' He heard the utter feebleness of his argument, and he resented that he should have to beg anybody for his son's sanity. He got up quickly from his chair. 'Please go,' he said to them. 'Thank you for coming. I'm sorry to put you to inconvenience. Is raining outside,' he added, with painful irrelevancy.

The door bell rang again, and one of the men made to go to the door, while the other restrained Rabbi Zweck from moving. Rabbi Zweck brushed his arm away. 'In my own house,' he said quietly, 'I can answer my own door.' But he did not try to leave the room. Instinctively he felt that there would be a battle in the hall, as losing a battle as the one he was trying to ignore in the kitchen. He waited for the doctor to return. With him came another man, Mr Angus, as he was introduced, with the terrifying appendage of Mental Health Officer. Mr Angus put out his hand to Rabbi Zweck, and squeezed it with obscene professional understanding. Rabbi Zweck backed away and slumped weakly on his chair. 'Is raining outside,' he said again.

The two doctors left the room. Mr Angus shut the door after them, and drew his chair to Rabbi Zweck's side. He put his arm on his shoulder, and knew that he could say nothing. It was never easy, his job, but dealing with the next-of-kin was the worst part of it. Some of his colleagues, he knew, revelled in the 'schadenfreude' of their work, but he was different. And he promised himself, once again, as he had done so often in the last ten years, that he would find himself some other kind of work. They sat together and there was nothing to do but listen to the noises outside Norman's door, and as they grew louder, Mr Angus moved his chair closer to the old man's, and gently stroked his arm.

'Get out,' Norman was yelling. 'What right have you to come into my room?'

'Open the door,' the doctor said gently. 'We just want to talk to you. You don't want us to force the door, do you? Now be a good boy.'

It was the word 'boy' that triggered off Rabbi Zweck's tears. He was a grown man, his son, and you called a grown man 'boy' only if you had contempt for him. 'He's not mad, is he, my son?' he whispered to Mr Angus. Mr Angus squeezed his arm. 'This is what's best for him. I promise you. It'll only be a few weeks, and he'll be out again. It'll all be over,' he said. He refrained from adding, 'until the next time'. He had dealt with lots of similar patients. He had comforted the stunned parents, or the weeping wives and children. By standing in front of doors, and wooing them with gentle lies, he had sincerely tried to camouflage the hideous paraphernalia of putting people away. It wasn't so bad when they went voluntarily. It was when they resisted, like this one was doing. That was the hell of it, not for the patient himself, but for those who were watching and could not bear it. 'When the doctors have seen him,' he said, 'I'll talk to him. I'll do what I can.'

There were so many things that Rabbi Zweck wanted to know. How would they force him to go? Would they use a strait-jacket? Would there be policemen at the door? Would he go in a white ambulance? And what kind of place was he going to? And was it full of madmen, of real *meshugoyim*, not like his son who was going to be better soon? But he daren't ask any of these questions. He did not want to acknowledge the situation. But it screamed at him from outside the door. A large resounding kick and 'We'll have to get the police if you don't let us in.'

'Tell them to go away,' Rabbi Zweck pleaded. 'Or let me talk to him.' He half rose to go to Norman's door. Norman would never forgive him. He sat down again and put his hands over his face, and rocking gently to and fro, with praying and weeping, he stilled himself into a semblance of calm. He heard Norman's door suddenly open, and again he started weeping at his son's surrender. He heard the doctors go inside, and shut the door behind them.

'He's better now – he'll be all right now,' he said to Mr Angus. 'They've given him a shock and he's better. It's just he

29

needed someone to teach him a lesson. Go home now, all of you.' He was offering a last-minute alibi, but his son had already confessed. Rabbi Zweck felt Mr Angus' hand leave his arm, and he knew he was alone in the kitchen.

He didn't want to think of what was happening in Norman's room. He couldn't even understand that it had anything to do with him. He was only conscious that it was raining outside, with a thin endless drizzle. He heard two men walk through the hall and out of the front door. He was glad they hadn't come to say good-bye to him. He just hoped they'd brought their umbrellas. He heard murmurings from Norman's room, and he recalled the same quality of murmuring from the dying-bed of his wife, and he sensed that a similar catastrophe awaited him.

'Papa,' Norman called from his room. His voice was desperate and imploring like a little boy's. It was a cry for immediate help and protection. It was a cry of physical pain, and Rabbi Zweck responded. Whatever had happened to his son, he would kiss it better, and tell him a story to keep his mind off the pain. He hurried to Norman's room. Mr Angus was sitting on the bed, looking at Norman helplessly.

'Papa,' Norman pleaded as his father came in. 'Tell this man to go away. People come here, strangers, and they come into my room, and they want to take me away. I haven't done anything Papa, tell them I'm all right. Don't let them take me away.'

The door bell rang, and Mr Angus went out quickly to open the door.

'They've come for me,' Norman said. 'Papa, Papa,' he beseeched him, 'don't let them take me.'

Rabbi Zweck held him in his arms. 'It's only for you to get better,' he said gently. 'I'll come with you,' he said, 'we'll go together.'

'No, no,' Norman screamed. He tore himself away from his father and looked at him in utter bewilderment. 'Papa?' he said again, as if to question his father's right to a son. 'You ... you can't.' He opened his eyes wide in sheer incredulity. He stared at his father without hate, without bitterness, only with complete and innocent refusal to believe what his father had said. It was a look that Rabbi Zweck would shoulder to his grave.

'Come along now.' A new figure, another stranger, this time in uniform, came into Norman's room. 'Let's go quietly, shall we,' it said. 'We don't want any fuss.'

'Look at them,' Norman was saying, 'they're taking me away, and you just stand there and don't say a word. Papa,' he said tenderly, 'what's the matter with you? Aren't you well? D'you want to go to bed? Shall I look after you?'

As he was talking, the uniformed stranger came up behind him and motioned Mr Angus to stand by his side. But Norman didn't feel their movement. 'He's not well,' he said to them without looking up. 'I must put him to bed and call the doctor.'

Rabbi Zweck looked into Norman's face and shuddered at the unwitting blackmail of his son's love and concern. Then, flinging his frail arms around him, he clutched him with a strength that Norman remembered from his mother's dying embrace. 'My father must be dying,' he said to the stranger.

'Come along now,' the man said, taking his arm.

'You'll need your mackintosh,' Rabbi Zweck sobbed. 'Is raining.'

Mr Angus and the stranger took Norman on either side, urging him to go along.

'Leave me alone,' Norman shouted. 'I've got to stay home and look after my father.'

The men were losing patience and they grabbed him and dragged him barefoot to the door. Rabbi Zweck saw his son's empty shoes on the floor. 'Put your shoes on, put your shoes on,' he sobbed. He couldn't bear to see them there, empty. The stranger picked up the shoes and kicked them towards Norman's feet. Norman slid into them helplessly, his bare shiny heels, sitting on the turned-down leather.

Rabbi Zweck followed them downstairs. From the back his son looked suddenly very old, his black thinning hair sticking out on each side, his dressing-gown hitched up by the men's grips, his pyjama-legs creased up to his knee. He was astonished to notice the amount of hair on his son's legs. And possibly for the first time in his life, he acknowledged his son as a grown man, an old man even, old enough, he thought, to die from natural causes.

There were two flights of stairs to the ground floor and into the back entrance of Rabbi Zweck's little grocer's shop and general store, which was the only way out into the street. Norman was struggling between the one man's grasp and the other's, but he said nothing, sickened by the injustice of it all. They reached the narrow entrance to the shop. Norman's dressing-gown cord trailed on the floor. Rabbi Zweck bent down and picked it up tenderly, as if he were carrying a bride's train. Folding the end in front of him, he followed the group into the shop.

Bella was serving a customer, while a group of women waited at the counter. Bella stared at the little procession. She knew she would have to raise part of the counter for them to get through, but she too, wanted no part in his going, and dared not let Norman see her contribution. But the customer who stood by the counter division, an unaccusable bystander, lifted the wood partition, and Bella inwardly blessed her for it. 'Must you go too?' she said to her father. Neither of them were concerned about the customers in the shop.

'Is much harder to stay,' Rabbi Zweck said.

The three of them had reached the door, and Norman, until now silent, swung round suddenly and faced the customers in the shop. 'I've got witnesses,' he shouted triumphantly, 'all of you, you're witnesses they're taking me away. They're putting me in a loony bin,' he screamed, horrified as the full meaning of his words struck him. 'You'll be sorry,' he shouted to no one in particular. 'I'll sue you, all of you. There'll be damages.'

Mr Angus and the stranger pulled him into the street, and Rabbi Zweck followed, still holding the cord of his son's dressing-gown. At the door of his shop, he turned to his customers. 'I'm sorry you should be embarrassed,' he whispered.

Bella stared after them. She saw the men handle her brother into the back of a black car, and then the stooped black back of her father as he stumbled in after them. She watched the car out of sight, then she turned back to her customers. 'It's raining outside,' she said.

3

The stranger was driving, his back on the alert. Norman sat on the back seat, pinned between Mr Angus and his father, neither of whom, for their own reasons, dared look at him or at each other. He was calmer now, though Rabbi Zweck thought he felt his own shoulders throbbing with his son's sobs. He had seen old men cry, and little boys, but never a man. He prayed that the hospital was not far away. Whatever awaited him there, he wanted it over and done with. Out of the window he saw young women shopping, and children, picking out the pavement lines with their toes. He remembered how Norman used to play the same game. He shifted in his seat. His stomach was troubling him. He was aware of a growing physical pain in his body, that seemed to have nothing to do with the horror in his mind. His back ached with a nagging drawing pain, and his stomach contracted from time to time in agonizing cramps. He was normally a healthy man, and he couldn't understand these sudden symptoms. He wondered whether Norman was in pain too. He turned to look at him. Norman smiled, and leaned forward, ostensibly to straighten the heel of his shoe. But suddenly, when both his keepers were off guard, he put one hand on the door handle and pressed it down. But it snapped back into position and he realized that it was locked from the outside. Not only the attempt, but the failure of it had been witnessed and it was that which humiliated him into a sudden manic urge to escape. He banged on the window. 'Help, help,' he cried. A few passers-by gazed at the demented face at the window.

'Are you all right back there,' the driver said without turning his head.

Norman was standing now, banging on the window, trying to claim the attention of passers-by.

'Stop a policeman if you see one,' Mr Angus ordered the driver.

'No, no,' Rabbi Zweck said. 'Let me try. Norman,' he pleaded, 'sit down, please, please, for my sake. Don't get the policeman,' he pleaded with Mr Angus. 'Let me try to manage him.'

Mr Angus had gripped Norman round the waist and was making an effort to get him on to the floor of the car. 'Grab his legs,' he shouted to Rabbi Zweck, but Rabbi Zweck couldn't. In his madness, his son had assumed a remote untouchability, which for Rabbi Zweck was almost holy. He watched helplessly as Mr Angus succeeded in felling Norman to the floor. Then Mr Angus sat back on his seat, and rested his two legs over Norman's body like a conqueror.

'Don't worry about the police,' Mr Angus told the driver. 'He'll be all right now.' He brushed down his suit with some annoyance, pressing his foot on Norman's stomach. 'Now shut up,' he said, 'you've been enough trouble already.' Even for those who dealt professionally with the mad, madmen had sinned, and were to be punished. Rabbi Zweck bent down and stroked his son's forehead. It was streaming with sweat, and he felt the fever through his fingers. 'He's got a temperature,' Rabbi Zweck said to Mr Angus accusingly.

'And that's not all he's got,' Mr Angus said.

The houses were disappearing behind them, and the car was soon travelling through a country road. Rabbi Zweck huddled into his coat, trying to isolate himself from his surroundings, shrinking deep into an anonymous pinpoint of a situation whose reality he could not fathom. But he stared at Norman all the time, pouring into his gaze all his love for his son that he hoped Norman would not misunderstand.

But Norman, lying on the floor, felt no part of him, nor even of himself as an object of his stare or of the offensive boot planted on his stomach. He stared at the roof of the car and the black rexine covering that bubbled and cracked in the corners. As he stared at it, it seemed to descend, embracing him like an easy winding-sheet for his own private and particular dying. That's what it was like, lying there, an opting out, a withdrawal from all his doubts, a retreat from his own and other's suspicions, a gentle turning away from all uncertainty. He closed his eyes and gave himself up wholly to the peace and the joy that invaded him. His father looked at his face, and watched the slow spreading of his son's smile. 'So long he's happy,' he thought to himself, and a great tenderness engulfed him. He nudged Mr Angus, inviting him to share his momentary relief. Mr Angus smiled at him. 'We're almost there,' he said, 'it'll soon be over.'

But Rabbi Zweck had momentarily forgotten their destination. He shivered at Mr Angus' reminder. The car was winding up a narrow country lane, with no signs of habitation on either side, isolated, remote, a foretaste of the greater quarantine.

Norman opened his eyes suddenly. He sensed the prison around him. He tried to get up, but Mr Angus' boot pressed more firmly on his stomach.

'Let me out,' he screamed.

'You'll be out soon,' said Mr Angus. 'We're almost there.'

Norman felt the swerving of the car as it turned through the wooded lay-out of the hospital. Then it stopped suddenly, so that Mr Angus had to embed his foot even further into Norman's stomach, to keep his own balance. For Norman, the sheer physical pain of it momentarily erased its cause, and the man behind the cause, and how the man came to be there and why. Norman knew that behind the pain lay a long uneasy history, partly forgotten but naggingly there. But for the moment, the pain was more than enough for him to deal with and he clutched his stomach as Mr Angus and the driver half dragged him out of the car.

'What's the matter? What's the matter?' the Rabbi cried, half in hope that at last, something genuine, something tangible could account for his son's aberrations. 'Is appendicitis,' he diagnosed triumphantly. He shouted his findings at the white-coated men who were approaching them down the hospital corridor. 'You must put him in hospital. Straight away.'

'We'll look after him. Don't worry,' a male nurse told him. 'They try all kinds of tricks to get out of here,' he went on chattily, as if Rabbi Zweck was connected with the new patient in some professional capacity.

'I'm his father,' Rabbi Zweck said.

'Come, sit down,' the nurse said gently. But Rabbi Zweck did not want to let Norman out of his sight. They reached the ante-room outside the main ward. The room was lined with tables, and pyjamaed, slippered men were carrying pots of tea and plates of bread and butter. They had the infinitely vulnerable look of men in pyjamas, helpless, exposed, unarmed. One of them, a bald-headed man, tapped Norman on the sleeve as he passed him by. A new face in the ward was always an excitement. It presented the possibility of variation on other people's day-to-day monotony of madness. You got weary of the man who insisted he was a snail, or the man who swallowed everything he laid his hands on. This new arrival might have something of a change to offer. ' 'Ullo mate,' the bald-headed man said. 'Christ is waiting for you. Put on your pyjamas and I'll take you to him.'

'Come off it, Harry. You need morning-dress to go and see Christ,' said another inmate with the pathetic humour of the mad taking the mickey out of the mad.

The bald-headed man shuffled off with his pot of tea, smiling to himself. Then, as an afterthought, he rushed back to Norman. 'They think we're mad,' he whispered aloud. 'But I don't care. Christ only receives mad people, so I don't want to be not mad.' He shouted this last to his tea-taking colleagues. Some laughed; others were too withdrawn into themselves even to hear him. He let go of Norman's sleeve. 'Hallelujah,' he shouted, crossing himself with his free hand. Then he skipped between the rows of tables. 'Hallelujah, I'm a bum, hallelujah, bum again,' he sang, until a nurse restrained him, patted his back and sat him down on a chair.

Norman's diminished area of sanity had suddenly become very acute. He looked at his father, embracing both him and his grotesque environment in one glance, and he said, 'Thank you for what you've done to me. Thank you.'

Rabbi Zweck gripped the nearest chair. The nurse helped him sit down.

'You've nothing to blame yourself for,' he said. 'You've done what's best for him.'

They led Norman into a little room off the tea-corridor, and

Rabbi Zweck saw the door close behind him. He stared at the stained white table-cloth in front of him. He was aware of a man taking the chair opposite. He saw his dirty-nailed hands place the bread and butter dish on the cloth, and slop the brown tea in the saucer back into the cup. On some of the bread and butter slices, Rabbi Zweck noticed a thin smear of raspberry jam. He was grateful for this minute concession to luxury, and he smiled at the man opposite him. He needed to talk to this man, this older man. He needed to tell someone about his son; he needed to leave a guardian for Norman for the duration of his stay. 'Is long you're here?' he asked timidly.

The old man did not answer.

Rabbi Zweck tried again. 'Are you going home soon?' he said.

The man bit into his sandwich and gulped his tea.

'Are you all right?' Rabbi Zweck asked.

The man rose from the table, his sandwich still half in his mouth and using his two hands to carry his tea, he walked purposefully down the corridor and disappeared into the ward.

'Leave me alone. There's nothing in my pockets.' Rabbi Zweck heard Norman screaming from behind the door. He got up automatically to go to his son's help, but as he rose, a nurse came forward to stop him. 'What are they doing to him?' Rabbi Zweck whispered.

'It's a routine check,' the arms said. 'It's no good if he's hiding some pills in his pockets, and taking them while he's here. We have to make absolutely sure.'

Rabbi Zweck nodded. He approved of the procedure. He just could not bear his son's humiliation. 'I must find the murderer who sells them to him,' he promised himself. 'Or else, he comes out of here and again he starts. I'll go home, I'll go through the drawers, I'll turn inside out everything, I'll find it, I'll find it . . .' he realized he was talking aloud, and when he looked up, he found that another man, a younger one this time, was sitting opposite him. The man's nails were clean and manicured, and he held his cup with one hand, while with the other he delicately ate a sandwich. He smiled at Rabbi Zweck. 'Does your son play chess?' the man asked. His voice was gentle and his accent well-heeled.

'Yes,' Rabbi Zweck said hopefully. Perhaps this man was someone of Norman's own class.

'That's good,' the man said. 'I haven't played a game for six months. That's when the last player left.'

'How long you are here?' Rabbi Zweck was almost afraid to ask.

'Six months, this time.'

'This time?'

'I was here before for a year.'

Rabbi Zweck wanted to find out what was the matter with him. Could he have the same as Norman? Was Norman going to be in and out of this place like this one?

The man raised his cup to his lips, and as he did so, the sleeve of his silk dressing-gown slipped almost up to his elbow. Around his wrist, Rabbi Zweck saw a circle of red scars, the suicide's bracelet. He shuddered.

'I'll look after your son,' the man was saying. 'Don't worry about him.'

'He's not a very good chess player,' Rabbi Zweck said. He was trying to withdraw the need for the man's surveillance. 'As a matter of fact,' he went on, 'my son Norman doesn't like the chess, except on his own to play. That he likes.' He was about to elaborate on his son's dislike of partnership, when the door at the end of the tea-room opened and he saw Norman, tamed, beaten, and barefoot, clutching the hand of the male nurse who had met them on arrival. He did not look back in his father's direction. He was lagging at the nurse's side as they entered the ward, like a child trailing his mother into the park. Rabbi Zweck stared after him and watched the tail end of his dressing-gown cord as it disappeared round the corner of the door. He didn't know what to do. He was afraid to go and see Norman, but he was afraid too, to leave. So he sat there, cursing his son's nameless supplier, and swearing aloud that he would track him down.

After a while, the nurse came out of the ward and walked towards him. 'You can see your son now,' he said, 'just for a little while.'

Rabbi Zweck hesitated. 'Don't worry,' the nurse said. 'He's

calm now. We've given him a sedative and soon he'll be asleep.'

'Did he say I should come?' Rabbi Zweck asked.

'Come and see him,' the nurse said, helping him up from his chair.

Rabbi Zweck was frightened. Supposing Norman didn't want to see him, and how could he refuse, in bed as he must be, and helpless? And what was there left between them that either of them could put into words? But he couldn't not go into the ward, and the nurse was already leading him. He didn't know what to expect behind the closed doors. While he had been waiting, he had seen men come out of there, all with the same expressionless face, all without hope, but hoping all the same.

The room was endless with beds. Ranged on each side with terrifying neatness, some occupied, some heaped with blanket-covered misery, and all in their way absolutely empty. Between the two rows of beds, shuffled slippered men, back and fore, to and fro, as if waiting at a trainless station. Rabbi Zweck wanted to go home. But he had already seen Norman, or rather the huddled shape of him in the bed half-way down the room. Though it looked like any other shape, contained, calm and empty, he knew, by the sudden stab of pain in his groin, that it was his son. The nurse dragged a chair to the side of the bed so that Rabbi Zweck could sit down, and there he left him, alone.

Rabbi Zweck touched the heap on the bed. 'Norman?' he said. 'Is Papa.'

There was no movement from under the blanket. Rabbi Zweck thought that perhaps Norman hadn't heard. He stood up and leaned over the heap. 'Norman,' he said again, 'is Papa.'

'Take me home,' Norman whispered.

Rabbi Zweck looked around him. The chess player was on his way towards them, carrying a board. Rabbi Zweck shook his head. 'Not now,' he whispered as the man approached. 'He wants to sleep.' The chess player shrugged, disappointed. He moved away slowly and joined the group of shufflers between the rows of beds.

'Norman,' Rabbi Zweck tried again.

Norman drew the blanket from his face. He had been sobbing.

'What did they do to you in that room?' Rabbi Zweck asked.

'You brought me here,' Norman said.

'Is for your good. The doctors say.' He himself didn't want to take the responsibility.

'But Papa, you told them they could take me. You could have stopped them. Take me home. Please,' Norman started crying.

Rabbi Zweck tried to be firm. He cradled Norman's head in his arms. 'Stay here a little,' he said. 'Just a few days. You'll go home today and you'll start again with the pills.'

'I won't, I won't,' Norman shouted. 'I promise. I won't touch them again. Never. I know what they do to me. I promise.' The tears welled from his swollen eyes, and it was more than Rabbi Zweck could bear. He began to wonder whether he had done the right thing. He even toyed with the idea of smuggling Norman out of there. He looked across at the opposite bed. He'd not noticed anybody there before, but now, a man sat there, bolt upright against the pillows, staring at him.

'What you looking?' Rabbi Zweck screamed at him. 'Is not your business.' He was in a frenzy of despair. 'Is my son,' he shouted. 'What you looking?'

The man continued to stare at him.

'What you looking?' Rabbi Zweck screamed at him again.

Norman sat up in bed. 'Sh, Papa,' he said. 'Take no notice. He's mad. They're all mad here. Take me home. Please,' he begged.

'I'll see the doctor,' Rabbi Zweck said. He knew he shouldn't have said it. Painful as it was, he had to leave his son in this place.

'Go and see him now,' Norman said. 'I'll wait here for you,' he said generously.

'Look,' said his father, 'you must stay. Is for your own good,' he went on helplessly. 'Perhaps not too long you'll stay. I'll ask the doctor.' He couldn't stop himself saying it.

'Go and ask him now,'

'On my way out, I'll ask him.'

Norman looked at him with hatred. 'I'll tell you something,' he said. 'I'm as sane as you are, whatever that means, but if I stay in this nut-house, even for a few days, I'll be mad as the rest of them. I promise you. You want me to go mad?' he said.

The nurse approached the bed and motioned Rabbi Zweck to leave. Rabbi Zweck was grateful that the nurse had come, but his sense of relief made him feel guilty. 'Good-bye, Norman,' he said, hating the weakness in himself. 'I should go now. They won't allow me any more. You should sleep.'

Norman went under his blanket.

'Good-bye, Norman,' Rabbi Zweck repeated.

There was no answer. Rabbi Zweck bent over and kissed the blanketed hump and the nurse gently led him away.

Outside the door, he asked to see the doctor. But as he was to learn in his subsequent visits, seeing a doctor in a mental home is a very hit and miss affair. You had to be on the spot at the right time and on the right day. Otherwise you had to make do with the male nurses, the infinite number of tranquillizer-trolley pushers who hourly plied their rounds of the beds, doling out substitute illusions, or oblivion. No, he didn't want to see a nurse, Rabbi Zweck said. He wanted to see a doctor.

'He's not here, and he won't be here till tomorrow.'

'Who shall I see then?' Rabbi Zweck asked timidly.

'You can see the nurse in charge.'

Rabbi Zweck was led into the room where Norman had first been taken. He was surprised to find it small and inoffensive, with a table, a couple of chairs, and a trolley of medicine. Behind the table sat a white-coated nurse. He rose as Rabbi Zweck entered and shifted a chair for him to sit down. Under the chair, Rabbi Zweck caught sight of one of Norman's shoes, turned down at heel, and empty. He began to cry, openly and unashamed. The nurse put his arm on his sleeve. 'He'll be all right,' he said. 'This is the worst time, especially for you.'

'How long he should stay?'

'I can't tell you,' the nurse said. 'The doctor will look at him tomorrow.'

'I shall come tomorrow?' Rabbi Zweck asked.

'It's better to leave it for a few days. You can ring up any time.'

'Where does he get them from?' Rabbi Zweck said. 'I'll find out, I'll ransack the house. I'll find who gives them to him.' He crumpled up on the chair hopelessly.

'Don't worry about that,' the nurse said. 'Let's get him over it first. He'll settle down after a few days. He'll even get to liking it here.'

Rabbi Zweck shuddered. He didn't want his son liking it here. He wanted him home without his silver fish, and a good son to him. 'At home he sees them,' he said tonelessly. 'Everywhere he sees them. He smells them, he hears them. They live with him. Why my son? My clever son,' he said, almost to himself.

The nurse leaned forward over the table. 'Rabbi,' he said softly, 'if your son went out into the garden, and came back and said, father, I've seen a burning bush, would you not bless him?'

He guided Rabbi Zweck to the door. In the corridor, the driver of the car was waiting for him. Mr Angus had disappeared, and Rabbi Zweck was the sole passenger on the long journey home. 'I'll ransack the house,' he said to himself, over and over again, and he kept hearing Norman's pleading voice to take him home.

The shop was empty when he arrived, and Bella was sitting behind the counter. She didn't want to talk about it and neither did her father. She tried to persuade him to go to bed, but he was restless. He trudged upstairs to the flat and, without taking off his coat, he went straight to Norman's room.

4

At first, Rabbi Zweck frantically opened every drawer, rummaging through their contents with feverish fingers. Then, exhausted, he sat down on the bed. He knew it was going to be a long job. There was no lack of material, and each scrap of paper might yield a clue, or a clue to clues of his son's murderer. Or perhaps there were many murderers, a clutch of assassins, their pockets lined with his son's craving.

When his wife, God bless her soul, was dying, she had leased the room, lock, stock and barrel, to Norman. All the papers that his wife had accumulated over the years, lay there still, disordered in their own time, but now, even more so by Norman's additions. In his initial scrummaging, Rabbi Zweck had caught sight of marriage papers, school reports, birth certificates, shuffled in disarray, with no respect to chronology. Yes, it would be a long job, and God knows what irrelevant yet painful material the search was likely to yield. He huddled himself into his coat. He felt his body cold. Sitting there on the bed, facing the ferreted drawers, he felt like a thief, and he began to hate himself for having volunteered for the job. A man had no right to invade another man's privacy, as he was doing, and the sheer immorality of his act sickened him. A man had to be dead before you could go through his pockets, and even then, the action was faintly treacherous. Yet it had to be done, and may God forgive him for his disloyalty. He hoped fervently that Norman was sleeping.

He got off the bed, and stared at the drawers. He would have to make a start. He knelt down and fingered through the bundles, looking for something that would least incriminate his son, that would least enter into his son's private life. Just to begin with, he promised himself, then he would tackle the job properly. Going through one of the drawers, he ignored

Norman's diaries and a bundle of letters. He dreaded having to go through those, so he shut his eyes and hid them at the back of one of the drawers. He hoped he'd never find them again. Then he came across a worn faded parchment. He laid the folded document on the floor, and as he opened it, it split slightly along the creases. He spread it out carefully. It was stamped and red-sealed with officialdom and he recognized it as his paper of naturalization. He smiled. He was pleased with his find. It had nothing to do with Norman. It was part of his own life, and safely nostalgic to investigate. He tried to order his memory so that it would recall the beginning of his story. Surrounded as he was by the chaos of neglected continuity, he wanted desperately to get one thing straight, himself and his beginnings in England, long before Sarah, God bless her, his wife, and Norman, God help him, his son. He wanted to shed himself of his married and paternal years, of the birth of his children and Sarah's passing. He wanted to peel off circumstance, to whittle himself down to the short legged stubborn pinpoint that would answer to the name of Abraham Zweck.

He spread his hand over the document, and concentrated on the ship that had brought him to England, gripping the rails to hold on to the recollection. In his state of sadness and anxiety, it was imperative to escape into his past, for his present was unbearable. He gripped the rails tightly. He had to hang on to them until the cold steel was real under his hands. And when he felt it, cold and undeniable in his grip, he was safely wrapped in his twenty-three years, almost fifty years ago, in sight of a new and frightening land.

The shore line sickened him. While out at sea, the reality of the new life that awaited him, and the remembrance of the severed ties at home in Lithuania, had both become meaningless. But now, faced with the shore, he experienced again the pain of departure, and the fearful anticipation of his arrival. He would never see his parents again. That much was certain. And they knew it too. His brothers, both married with children, had found it harder to leave, and they had sent him, the baby, to scout the lay of the land, and eventually to send for them. He

44

shivered at the responsibility, with a slight resentment at their expectations.

He turned his back on the approaching coastline. He looked down at himself. His small black boots and white wool socks protruded untidily beneath his long black coat. The lowest button was undone, and fell open on the white gaiters. The shadow of his wide-brimmed black hat crossed the tip of his boots, and as he bent forward, his side-locks too cast their shadows, and he rocked his head to and fro, trying to fit the shadow hat on his boots and the curls alongside. At last he struck a position where the whole picture was symmetrical, his boots in the centre, his shadow hat fitting squarely across the toe-caps, bracketed by the side-locks on each side. He held the picture steady, until a pair of naval boots moved on to it, and blocked it out. Abraham Zweck looked up and saw the officer smiling at him. 'Another half an hour and we'll be landing,' he said. Abraham Zweck raised his eyebrows. It was the safest movement to make if you didn't understand the language. It could mean both 'yes' and 'no' and the nuances of 'perhaps' and 'nevertheless'. The officer passed on, and Abraham Zweck turned back to look at the shore line which had suddenly crept up behind him, solid and irrefutable.

He put his hand in his inside pocket, checking once again on the slip of paper that was his sole contact in the strange world that approached him. He looked at the crumpled sheet. The name was Rabbi Solomon, and the address, number 16 of an unreadable street followed by the letters E.2. He went down the ladder steps that led to the bottom deck. He had left his parcels there, stacked in a corner while he had gone to the upper deck for air. He went to collect them, and as he picked them up, the string slipped and the brown paper gaped with its lining of Russian newspapers. He tried to push both sides together, but the string slipped completely, and he found himself surrounded by rolled socks, woollen underwear, his prayer shawl, prayer books, and an odd white gaiter. He shook the paper to free whatever might be left inside. The other gaiter fell out, and that was all. He shivered with humiliation. A poor Jew he was indeed, who could not even pack a parcel, an occupation that was a forte amongst his people. He retrieved the prayer book, kissing it, and stood up and looked around him. Yes, that was all he had. That was all he was, his body and its means of function. As the parcel had gaped open, it had undressed him, and as he grew conscious of the people staring at him, he felt ashamed, not of his poverty, but of his nakedness. He put a hand on his crotch, gripping the black alpaca of his coat, and he bent down to retrieve the rest of his person. He took his time about it, wanting the crowd to disperse. Then he sat on the deck and retied his parcel securely, and when it was done, he followed the passengers down the gangway.

He followed them to London, through the customs and on to the train with an occasional raising of the eyebrow, and without uttering a single word. He couldn't remember how he'd reached the address in the east end of London. All he recalled were people staring at him, in the street and on the strange tramcars, and often he checked on the string of his parcel to see that it was secure. Then gradually, people stared no longer. He saw other men, like himself, white-gaitered, long-coated, and carrying parcels. One even acknowledged him in his mother tongue. There were little shops too, like the ones back home, with barrels of herrings and black olives standing outside. He was happy for the first time since he'd left home.

His confidence grew and he entered one of the shops, and showed his piece of paper to the man behind the counter. The man looked up and spoke to him in Yiddish. Where had he come from? Who was he? And his father? What business was he in? Yes, things were getting worse, he knew. Every month, more and more were coming from the *Heim*. And things here not so good either. Antisemitism? Plenty. What d'you want? Where there's Jews, is anti-semitism. Do *I* make a living? Four daughters I've got. A living I've got to make. And how will you do, my boy? What living will you make? A Rabbi you want to be? Not enough Rabbonim we've got already. Well, everyone to his own *geschäft*. The man stopped suddenly, and stared at the stranger. Then, lifting the division of the counter, he said, 'Come in. A glass lemon tea you should have. Reb Solomon lives a stone's throw from here. My daughter will take you.'

The kitchen was immediately behind the counter, and there

they were, the four of them, and all alike from front and behind, turning away and giggling together. 'Sadie, Sarah, Leah and Rachel,' their father said, ticking off his progeny. 'A glass lemon tea for our visitor.'

They all headed for the samovar that was in the centre of the table. One of them smiled and it was to her that Abraham Zweck gave his heart. Immediately and eternally. She was about his age, a little younger perhaps.

'Which one are you?' he asked in Yiddish. The girls giggled together.

'Goyim, they are my daughters. Only a mouthful of Yiddish between them. Sarah,' he shouted, 'tell the gentleman your name.'

She nodded her head. Yes, that was it, what her father had said. But she blushed with the effort to identify herself.

Abraham Zweck took the tea that one of the others had handed to him. Everything was happening so quickly. Up until a few minutes ago he had been a stranger, surrounded by all that was alien, laughed at, followed and humiliated. And suddenly, others had become like him, as it was at home, with the same clothes and language, with the same shops, the same struggle, and the same marriageable daughters. He felt a great sense of arrival. He put a lump of sugar in his mouth and sucked the tea noisily. Just as it was at home.

'A Rabbi you shouldn't bother with,' the father was saying. 'For you,' he said, weighing him up as if after years of acquaintance, 'business is better. Your own business, you marry, you have a family. No troubles.' He was silent for a moment, taking stock of his own situation. He was no recommendation for his own advice. But he rallied quickly. 'Specially with a wife to help,' he went on. 'Poor Chayala, when the girls were babies, she passed away. Another wife I should have taken,' he mused, 'but it's never the same. Forget already the *Rabbonischkeit*,' he almost shouted. 'A business you should find. Your own business. Sarah,' he called, 'another glass tea for the gentleman.'

They talked. Abraham's town, his family, their problems. It was a familiar story. They were all the same, the *städtels* in the East, and now in the West too, bred from the same root. The shopkeeper's Yiddish was fluent, but it was punctuated by the occasional English word, which, by the gist of the general meaning, Abraham Zweck was able to understand. In his first years in England, this was the way he was to pick up the language, collecting all these odd English throw-outs, for which the speakers knew no Yiddish equivalent. Words like wardrobe, electric fire, conservative. Hundreds of single words that together gave Abraham Zweck a great vocabulary, but little language. His conversation became like his friends', only in reverse. He would use Yiddish throw-outs in the brackets of his halting English. The people of the neighbourhood understood him as he did them, and they learnt more Yiddish from his speech. It was a mutual linguaphone.

Sarah brought in the tea. Abraham smiled his thanks at her but she turned away, shyly. Her father patted her arm as she left the table. 'My eldest,' he said. 'Like a little mother she is. Isn't that right, Mammele?' he called after her. She giggled with her sisters. The shopkeeper caught Abraham looking at her. He leaned over the table. 'The best, she is, the best,' he whispered.

They drank their tea. Abraham once more asked directions to Reb Solomon's house.

'Sarah will show you,' the shopkeeper said. 'Is not far from here. Sarah, go get your coat.' He turned to Abraham, and switching to Yiddish, said, 'You want to go upstairs, perhaps?'

Abraham wanted to stay and watch Sarah. But he was curious to see how closely a Jewish upstairs in England corresponded with his family's at home. 'Yes, he would go upstairs,' he offered.

The shopkeeper leaned over the bannister and directed him. When he was out of sight, Abraham wandered through the rooms. In one of them, he leaned against the door, and stared at the chest of drawers opposite him.

Rabbi Zweck shuddered. There it was, still there, fifty years older, and still full of Sarah's things. He re-focussed his eyes, and what had, in his remembrance, been 'there', now suddenly in his awakening, became 'here'. Yes, this was the room in the house behind the shop that Sarah had inherited from her old father. He looked away from the chest to the bed, then to the pulled-out drawers and the terrible recollection of what he was doing.

'Ach,' he moaned, folding the naturalization certificate into its original creases. He hadn't come very far since his arrival almost half a century ago. Out of the window, he could see the side-door of the synagogue, and a group of small children coming out of their Hebrew lessons. He had probably taught their grandparents, in the same little ill-ventilated rooms next to the beadle's lodge. He had probably married their parents, joining them beneath the marriage canopy according to the laws of Moses and Israel. For forty years he had served in that synagogue, first as a pupil Rabbi, then as a fully-fledged teacher and minister, and then later on, as the congregation fell off, doubling as a cantor. The Hebrew class was now only a trickle of children, and who knew who and where they would marry? He thought of his daughter Esther, who had taught classes there too, and he shuddered at the thought of whom and how she married. He went over to the window. It was only a few steps from his shop to the door of the synagogue, and within its span lay his life's activity. Forty years as a Rabbi, then only to cross the road to his retirement as a help to Sarah in the shop, and he scanned the tiny compass in which so much sadness had gathered.

He hoped again that Norman was sleeping. He looked around him, at the cluttered drawers, and the naked privacy of his wife and son. 'Ach,' he murmured again, 'if he had seen a burning bush, like the nurse said, *takka*, I would have blessed him. But silver-fish.' He shuddered, and taking off his shoes, he climbed wearily on to Norman's bed, hesitating for a moment between Norman's side, and Sarah's, and then, as if acknowledging their equal and terrible sadness, he lay across the bed, and absorbed them both.

5

Norman was woken by the pain. He knew only one way of staving it off, and the thought of the floor-board underneath his bed comforted him even before he opened his eyes. But something bound him to the bed, the fear that some change had taken place, the suspicion that the floor-board had moved, or had been finally nailed down. He shuddered. He dared not open his eyes, and he tried in the dark to confirm or deny the change that he so dreaded. He felt the sheets. They were stiff and rough to his touch. But perhaps Bella had changed them and they were new. He stroked the pillow. That too was starched, but that too could be accounted for. Gingerly he stretched one leg to embed his toe in the security of the division of his mother's bed. Slowly he urged it outward, and stopped where the division should have been. He felt the cold steel of the bedframe. He shivered. He had to face it. He was not in his own bed.

He clasped his hand over his heart to still its fearful beating. He owed it to his body to find some reason for the change. Himself, he could cope with, but he needed to hoodwink his heart. 'You were ill last night,' he said to himself, 'and Bella carried you into the spare room with the little bed.' That was it. But he still had the problem of getting back to his room and the floor-board. But perhaps his father was sleeping in there. He would wait. Yes, it was easy to wait with your eyes closed, knowing that the floor-board was only two doors away. But the pain racked him. He would have to open his eyes and get out of bed. But first, he slithered off the bed, his eyes still closed. As his feet touched the cold lino, he knew with fearful certainty that he was not at home. Home was carpet, home was infested edge to edge, home was other people's blindness from wall to wall. He sat on the bed and opened his eyes wide, trying to control his panic. A male nurse was approaching him, wheeling the tranquillizer trolley. He stopped by Norman's bed, and taking two pink pills from a bottle on his cart, he reached out to the bed-table for a glass. He filled it with water and crossed to Norman's side. Then holding out the tablets, he said, 'You'll feel better when you've had these.' His voice was gentle. It had dispensed with the white-coated 'good mornings and how are we feeling today'. It was an immediate recognition of Norman's fear. 'Take them,' he went on, 'then I'll bring you some tea.'

Norman looked at the pink tablets in the palm of the nurse's hand.

'That's not my colour,' he said curtly.

'It's your colour while you're here, I'm afraid,' the nurse said, adding a little laugh to soften his undeniable authority.

'Pink,' Norman scoffed. 'No, thank you. You're not pulling pink ones on me.' He'd had them before, the pink ones. Dr Levy, more than once, had throttled him with pink. He called them tranquillizers, but Norman knew jolly well what they were. They were drugs that made him blind to his silver-fish, and Levy was trying to make an addict out of him. They were drugs that sent his fish away, so that his father and Bella could say, 'I told you so. I told you they were never there.' 'Pink,' he mocked again, 'the be-a-good-boy colour, the stop-driving-me-mad colour. The get-rid-of-the-evidence colour. No thanks, you have them. Be my guest.'

He heard his voice breaking with the pain that racked him, and he turned away from the nurse. He didn't want this stranger to see his helplessness. 'Haven't you any white ones?' he pleaded.

'Take them,' the nurse said and he took Norman's hand and fitted his fingers round the glass. 'They're for the pain,' he added.

Anything, anything for the pain. Even pink. Norman took the tablets without turning round. Their colour humiliated him. If he stared at them long enough, they would turn to white. He would will them white, and into the kick, the great inde-scribable kick that white fed him. But that was long ago, he confessed to himself. He had to acknowledge that of late, the kick had become describable, diluted and mundane. And the woman, and the loving that white had provided, that too, was long ago, and the appetite had fled. He swallowed the pills without bothering with the water. He'd never given the white ones the indignity of liquid, especially lately when it was as much as he could get and as quickly as he could get it, solid and uncontaminated by watery accompaniment. But oh, for what little return. 'No, no,' he chided himself, now was no time for remorse, now was no time for turning over new leaves. 'I've got to fight them. They're wrong.'

'You're wrong . . .' he turned to the nurse, but he had gone.

The ward was stirring. The patients, lately come from sleep, were tranquillized once more. Opposite him a man beckoned, the man, Norman remembered, who had stared at his father the night before, and who probably the whole night had stared across to Norman's bed, as he stared still. Norman went over to him. The man was holding the pills in one hand, while he beckoned continually with the other. Norman grasped his hand.

'What colour are yours?' he demanded.

The man opened his palm and the offensive pink was already smudged in the sweat of his hand. He reached for the glass of water which the nurse had left on his side-table. Then he threw the tablets in the glass and tossed the lot down the sink. Then he put the glass down and wiped his hands of the whole business.

'You must have *some* colour,' Norman said desperately.

'Is white a colour then?' the man said.

'God is good, God is good,' Norman whispered, and he dropped his head on to the man's hand. 'Please, please,' he begged.

The man lifted Norman's head with one hand, and the other he thrust down the bedclothes. Then withdrawing his hand he relaid Norman's head in place. 'Shut your eyes and open your mouth,' he said.

Norman lifted his head, glanced at the man's clenched fist, and looked furtively around the ward. The nurse and his trolley were safely down the other end. 'Let me see,' Norman said.

The man opened his palm, and inside lay one white tablet. 'That's for you,' he said generously.

Norman stared at the tablet, then at the man, then back to the tablet in his hand. What struck him most, was not its comforting colour but its terrible isolation. Not for many years had Norman seen one pill on its own. His daily ration was an increasing handful, uncountable. On its own, the tiny white spot seemed monstrous in its effrontery. How dare anyone underestimate his capacity to such a humiliating extent. If nothing else, a man had a right to his own dignity. He looked back at the man and laughed. 'Who d'you think you are?' he said. 'A doctor?'

'I'm the Minister of 'Ealth,' the man said. 'You can 'ave that one for nothing.'

There was hope, still hope. 'Is there more for money,' Norman asked.

'I s'pose you know it's against the law,' Minister said. '*Their* law. Those lunatics outside.' He knelt up on the bed. 'May I quote,' he said, assuming his ministerial voice. 'May I quote my opposite number in the shadow cabinet. The outside cabinet,' he added, needing to make himself clear. 'Amphetamines,' he said, rolling the word off his tongue with the agility of a pusher, 'amphetamines is as dangerous as the hard stuff, and the hard stuff is against the law.' He slouched down on his bed. 'In other words, mate, you and me, being as we are on the white kind, the amphetamine kind, you and me are law-breakers. On the outside,' he added. 'But in this place, where I 'ave the honour to 'old office for as long as there is a government, the only thing against the law, apart from my lousy Mum, is not 'aving the money.'

'How much is it?' Norman asked.

'A quid a day. You can 'ave as much as you want.'

Norman could hardly believe his good fortune. At home, it had cost him more than twice as much, and then only for a limited supply. He smiled as he recalled his father's leave-taking. 'It's for your own good,' he had said, and how right he had been. He looked around the ward, and had thoughts of permanent tenancy. Why not? There was a life here, other wards, other people, gardens, women, no family, and above all, unlimited white. He slipped the tablet into his mouth as a token gesture to assure his fretting stomach that more was on the way. Then he remembered that he had arrived in this place moneyless, in pyjamas. Again panic seized him. He turned to the man on the bed. 'What's your name?' he asked. He felt that were they to have some kind of relationship, an exchange of names was indispensable. 'Mine's Norman,' he said.

'I told you. I'm the Minister of 'Ealth.'

Norman put out his hand, surprised by the automatic respect he felt for the man. 'Then may I call you Minister?' he said.

'At your service.'

'Then,' Norman hesitated, 'Minister, may I have some white on account. I arrived here in pyjamas.'

'We 'ave a provision for that,' Minister said, 'since most of us arrive in what you may call our night attire. Cash on delivery or a ten per cent interest charge for an account.'

Norman had no idea how he was to come by the money, but it was a secondary consideration. 'Yes,' he said, 'I agree to the terms. I'll get you the money tomorrow.' He held out his hand.

'Not now,' Minister said. 'They're in my desk at the office. I'll bring them along later.'

'Of course,' Norman said, again with the ready acceptance of the man's fantasy. 'But will you be long?'

'After breakfast,' he said, 'you and me shall dine on white together.'

Norman went back to his bed. He turned to look back at Minister and found him staring at him. As an afterthought, Norman shouted across the ward, 'How long have you been here?'

Minister continued to stare at him. 'How long?' Norman asked again.

'Six years, on and off,' one of the patients offered. 'He's been here for six years.'

Norman shivered. For a moment, he'd had a strange vision of himself in Minister's cold and distant stare. He recalled his thoughts of permanent residence, and quickly he decided against it. He never wanted to stare like Minister, no matter how inexhaustible his white supply. 'Six years,' he muttered to himself. He had to get out of this place, and quickly. He got up and strode across the ward. The nurse in charge was standing idly by the door. Norman went straight up to him. 'I want to go home,' he said. 'Let me have my things.'

The nurse straightened and took him by the arm. 'Have you taken your pills?' he asked. The arm was urging Norman towards his bed.

'I've had my pills,' he said. 'Pink ones. It seems we all have pink ones here.' He heard something new in the tone of his voice that surprised him. It had suddenly and quite voluntarily become upper-class. It helped him to put some distance between himself and the nurse who was so politely yet so authoritatively ordering him to his bed. He shook his arm free. 'I can go alone,' he said with great dignity. 'I'm perfectly all right,' he added. 'I shall go to bed and wait for my tea.'

The nurse relinquished his hold and returned to his sentry post at the door of the ward. Norman lay on his bed. Minister was still staring, and Norman abdicated with a faint smile. The stare did not flicker. Norman settled back on his pillow and let the pain tear through him. Until the after-breakfast white, he would busy himself with plans, plans to escape, and until the escape, plans to get hold of some money.

6

'*You* ring them up, Bella,' Rabbi Zweck said.

'There's no point in ringing so soon. He hasn't been there long enough for there to be any change.'

'Do me a favour, Bella. Go to the phone.'

They had been sitting at the breakfast table since six-thirty. Both of them, neither of them having slept. Each in their separate rooms, they had waited for the first glimmer of light, and when it came, they slipped stealthily from their beds, neither wanting the other to know of their anguish. They had confronted each other on the landing. Neither referred to the earliness of the hour, yet both felt trapped red-handed in their suffering.

'You go first,' said Rabbi Zweck nodding towards the bathroom.

'You go,' Bella said. 'I'll wait.'

They looked at each other positively avoiding the unmentionable. Then Rabbi Zweck could contain himself no longer. 'Is too early to phone, already?' he said timidly.

'Wait until after breakfast,' Bella said. 'You should go back to bed anyway. You haven't slept all night, I can see.'

'Sleep. Who should sleep?' Rabbi Zweck muttered to himself as he went to the bathroom. Inside, he felt sick. He leaned over the towel rail. He was conscious of a movement in his chest that seemed to stutter its way down to his stomach. It was not painful. In fact he drew some relief from it in his curiosity to find out how the movement would end. Then it settled, with ease, in his groin. He heard Bella in the kitchen and the sound of teacups and the kettle. The pale sun limped through the bathroom window and he ran the water and felt its warmth through his fingers. He heard himself humming through his beard, without wondering what he had to sing about. Norman's torment knocked at his whole being, yet there was a sense of peace inside him. He used it to pray, knowing that it would not last. Then he washed himself but took no joy in the freshness, and the sun was like any sun on any morning. He went into the kitchen. 'What time is it?' he said.

'A quarter to seven.'

'In hospitals is always somebody by the telephone. Ring please, Bella.'

'But Norman will be sleeping. The doctor won't have seen him yet.'

'Yes,' Rabbi Zweck said, 'you're right. Let him sleep a little. Is sleep he needs. Lots of sleep.'

He drank his tea noisily. He wanted to talk to Bella and he wanted Bella to talk to him. He wanted her to give him something to hope for, although he knew he couldn't accept it. And Bella in her turn, wanted talk, but feared it. And both of them hoped that if you didn't talk about a matter, that matter would cease to exist. After all, they had, by constant reference to it, kept it alive. Perhaps, Bella had often thought, they themselves had contributed to it, had in fact sparked it off. All those great expectations, they'd had of him. All that infant prodigy stuff, with him in short trousers till his beard started to grow, and her in those white socks to clinch the illusion. She didn't want to think about it. She felt guilty of the part she inevitably played in her brother's madness, and the part played indeed by the whole family. Norman and his whole life had been an event for them all, it was something that had happened to *them* and had ultimately nothing to do with Norman at all. Norman might be in an asylum, but it was they, the two of them around the table, who were in crisis, because their event had gone sour. They had elected Norman for their scapegoat, each in their own way, her father, her mother, her sister and herself, and now the backlash was on them. Norman was in a nut-house, asserting his rights, the right not to have been chosen. For a moment she saw Norman alone, without sisters or parents, and she saw him whole and sane.

She turned to pour her father more tea. Something to do, something to kill the time which would soon, in the course of the dreadful day ahead, become unkillable.

'What time is it?' Rabbi Zweck asked again.

'Ten to seven.'

'Too early still,' he said.

'Go back to bed, Poppa,' Bella tried to persuade him.

'What should I do in bed?' He got up and went to the telephone. His hand rested on the receiver. He would leave it there until it was decently late enough to phone. He kept asking the time until Bella gave him her watch. He refused. It would have eliminated all conversation between them. 'You keep it,' he said. 'Tell me when it's eight o'clock.'

Nevertheless, at five-minute intervals, he asked the time again, and his question and her answer were enough to keep the matter of Norman spoken and alive between them. Bella managed to get him back to the kitchen. She tried to get him to eat something, but he had no stomach for it. They sat opposite each other, looking into their cups. They heard the milkman deposit his bottles downstairs.

'So late it is, already?' Rabbi Zweck asked.

'Eight o'clock,' Bella said.

'Is late enough,' he said, getting up. At the telephone, he stopped. He couldn't do it. He was afraid. He turned to Bella. '*You* ring them up,' he said.

She knew she would have to do it eventually. She couldn't let him do it. She saw how frightened he was. Yet she resented again her hopeless burden. Why could they not reap at least a little advantage from his absence. Why not an hour or two's holiday from the whole sorry business. 'Why don't you phone?' she said, horrified and helpless in the face of her own cruelty.

'On the telephone, I'm not so good,' he said. '*You* ring, Bella,' he pleaded.

She dialled the number. She wished her father would move away from the phone, and there was indeed nothing better that Rabbi Zweck wanted to do. He was afraid of knowing what he dreaded to know, yet he was still Bella's father and he could afford to show no fear.

'Finish your tea on the table,' Bella said, trying to make it easier for him.

'Yes, that's right,' he said gratefully, 'is not good, cold tea.'

He went back to the kitchen and half closed the door. He

heard the number ringing, and stretching out his foot, he pushed the door gently shut. He heard Bella's voice, but not her words. He hesitated, then moved to the door, and opened it very slightly. 'Good,' he heard Bella say, and 'Good', again. His heart leapt with hope. He opened the door with more confidence. 'I should go see him today?' he yelled into the hall. He shut the door quickly, dreading the reply. He heard Bella's voice and the intermittent silences, until the final click of the phone. He opened the door for her. 'Well?' he said.

She was smiling. 'Everything's fine,' she said. 'They're very pleased with him. He had a good night, and he's settling down well.' She spoke quickly as if fearing to forget the verbatim report.

'What did they say?' Rabbi Zweck wanted a repetition.

'He's fine,' Bella paraphrased. 'He's settling down.' She was relieved that someone else had the responsibility. But Rabbi Zweck wasn't too pleased with the settling down. He'd seen the place. Bella hadn't, and it was no place to get used to and settle down in. 'Is that all they said?' he asked.

'He's well,' Bella repeated, 'he's had a good night and he's settling down.' Suddenly in her own repetition of the bulletin, she heard its falseness; she saw it being read off a prompter by the nurse in charge. Well, a good night, settling down. It was a formal stereotyped answer to all phone calls. Or perhaps an alternative. Bad. A restless night. Refuses to settle. Suppose, Bella wondered, the patient had died. Was there a prompter for *that* telephone call? But what did she expect after all. That he was off the pills for ever and sorry for all the trouble he had caused, deeply sorry, on his knees sorry, and ready to live a new life and repent it all?

'Did you ask I should go and see him?' Rabbi Zweck said timidly.

'They said you should leave it for a few days.' She hadn't asked. She didn't want her father going there. Let Norman be on his own a little, a problem to other people. Let *him* suffer a little for a change. She was allowed to have such thoughts after all. She only had to look at her father to entertain them.

Rabbi Zweck was half relieved that he was not allowed to go. He vaguely suspected that Bella hadn't asked, and he was grateful to her, and happy to let the doubt lie acknowledged between them. 'So he's well,' he said. 'Is good, he's well. He'll be better. He'll finish with the pills. Dr Levy was right. Is the best thing we could have done.' He was almost happy with the situation, and the fact that everything was under control. The slightest encouragement from any source generated a tremendous optimism in him. 'I'll have a big breakfast,' he said, and Bella was glad to make it for him.

'I'll go in the shop today, Bella,' he said. 'Give you a rest.'

He didn't want to go back to the search. Why should he not take a day off from it all? And perhaps if they cured him, the search wouldn't be necessary. What was the point in asking for trouble. No. He'd leave it for today. He'd spend his time in the shop.

The shop was a refuge, for Bella too, and she dreaded a day in the flat. But she couldn't refuse her father's offer. But she was frightened by Norman's unpresence. She herself felt strangely paralysed without him, as if her whole purpose had been removed. Her father was already at the door. She knew and understood his haste. 'You'd better take a scarf with you,' she said. 'It can get chilly down there.'

'I'll be all right,' he said opening the door, 'I'll turn the fire on if I get cold.'

She wanted to detain him. She had always taken her father's dependence on her for granted, but now that he was going, and with such confidence, she knew that she could not manage without him, or at least without his needs, which together with Norman's, were her sole means of sustenance. Now she was alone in the flat, and she turned from the door, and away from Norman's room, and away from the kitchen, and away from each door, until she had turned full circle. She rushed to the front door in time to see her father turn the corner of the stair. 'Call me if the shop gets full,' she shouted after him.

'I'll manage,' he shouted back at her. He sounded almost happy.

7

As he raised the shutters over the shop door, he saw Mrs Golden waiting outside. It was unusual to have a customer so early. Then he remembered that Mrs Golden had been in the shop the day before and had witnessed Norman's departure. She had returned panting for the latest bulletin. The sight of her sickened him. He didn't need her veiled sympathy. He didn't want any kind of reminder of yesterday. Yet she'd been Sarah's, God rest her soul, closest friend, especially in her last days when she had loved her enough to want to go before her. For Sarah's sake he smiled and let Mrs Golden into the shop. She followed him as he trundled around the counter. Then once in position, behind the dividing board, he looked up and acknowledged her.

'Mrs Golden, you want something?'

She drew a piece of paper out of her bag and handed it to Rabbi Zweck. This too was not Mrs Golden's custom. Mrs Golden never knew exactly what she wanted. It was up to the shop assistant to suggest things to her to jog her memory. The suggestion of sugar would trigger off the need for tea, or butter for bread. Matches was a purchase she always forgot; there seemed no other commodity that Mrs Golden associated with it. But, today, all her needs were written neatly in a column, matches included. Rabbi Zweck shuffled around the shop collecting the items, and bringing them back one by one to the counter. Mrs Golden watched him, but neither said a word to the other. When Rabbi Zweck had collected the items together, he added up the bill on a piece of wrapping paper. 'One pound, three and twopence?' he said, looking up. She took two pound notes out of her bag and handed them to him. He gave her the change silently. Then she collected her purchases and put them one by one into her shopping bag. She turned on her way to the door.

Rabbi Zweck was angry. Hers was such a pointed silence, and he wondered generously whether she was sparing his feelings. Suddenly he decided he didn't want his feelings spared. 'Mrs Golden,' he shouted after her, 'why don't you say something?'

Mrs Golden came back to the counter. 'I thought perhaps you didn't want I should speak.'

'You have something to say?' Rabbi Zweck said angrily, 'say it then.'

'Nothing,' she murmured and turned to go away again.

'He's getting better,' Rabbi Zweck called after her.

Mrs Golden turned back once again, and settled down in the customer's chair. 'Thank God,' she said. 'Of course he'll get better. What else should he get?' She seemed against her will to have put an end to the conversation, and she was at a loss as to how to continue. She looked to Rabbi Zweck for a contribution.

'He'll be out soon,' he said.

'That's good.' Mrs Golden could find no more to say. Somehow they had both managed to by-pass the cause, the effects, the symptoms and the diagnosis, each of them subjects of gossip and speculation. Now all had been said. He was getting better. Soon he would be home. Such facts were not discussable. Yet Mrs Golden didn't want to leave, and she felt too, that Rabbi Zweck wanted to detain her.

'Stay a little, Mrs Golden,' he said. 'I'm not so busy.'

He had always called her Mrs Golden. Sarah, as well, although they had known her since they were married. In fact, as Rabbi Zweck tried to recall, he had entirely forgotten Mrs Golden's first name. He could remember Mr Golden. He was Lewis, Lou, they used to call him. He'd been dead now for five years, and perhaps Mrs Golden would have to die before Rabbi Zweck could remember how she was called.

'You remember,' he said to her, 'the early days, when the children were young, with your children, we went so often out. You remember the picnics we went together?'

'I remember the picnics,' she said. Then taking her turn, she said, 'You remember we all went to the Yiddish theatre? Remember?'

'I remember,' Rabbi Zweck said. His move. 'You remember the school concerts? Remember?'

Mrs Golden remembered that too. The theatre, the picnics, the concerts, separately and by association, they triggered off total recall, and they sat together remembering it all, and needing each other's silence.

'What made him like this?' Mrs Golden suddenly asked. For whatever she remembered, it was always around the figure of Norman that the recollection took place. And probably for Rabbi Zweck too. Because he was not surprised at her question. He had asked it of himself so many times. It was a question that had to be asked repeatedly. Just asked, and asked enough, all answers were superfluous.

'He's getting better,' he said quickly. 'This morning, I spoke to the doctor. Bella spoke. Very well, the doctor said he is. Is getting better,' he repeated, alarmed at the hollowness in his voice.

'Of course he gets better,' Mrs Golden said. 'But what made him like this. Such a clever boy he was. What made him like this?'

She was not grilling Rabbi Zweck. She wanted him to be able to talk about it.

'Is getting better,' he said again. He sat down on the high stool behind the counter. It was a gesture of helpless abdication. 'Yes, you're right, such a clever boy he was.'

'You remember . . . ?' Mrs Golden started, and Rabbi Zweck was glad of yet another souvenir. While it lasted it cancelled out the present situation. It was only when it was over that the souvenir was faced as something that had once been and would never be again.

'You remember . . .' Mrs Golden went on. Her storehouse was inexhaustible. Her efforts to take Rabbi Zweck's mind off Norman, in his present state, by placing it fairly and squarely on Norman as he used to be, were unflagging. 'You remember his first case, in the courts, and him there with his gown on and wig, looking like a pretty girl. We all went, you remember, Sarah, God bless her, with a new hat, brown it was, with feathers, my Lou, God bless him too, and the Teitlebaums and the Greenbergs and the Schwartz, the whole street, you remember.

And how he won. Oi, how he won.' She aimed at each word separately, picking them off with her tongue like single bulls-eyes. 'With his beautiful talk,' she remembered, 'such a speech he made. Such a clever boy he was.'

Rabbi Zweck caught himself smiling only when the smile faded from his face. The recollection of Norman's first triumph could only lead to the sad memory of his career's decline and the shameful humiliation of his last stand at the bar. Rabbi Zweck knew that Mrs Golden was already mourning it in her mind and he did likewise, because it was an event that he had to recall again and again until he could come to terms with it, laugh at it even – such a joke it was – until perhaps the shame of it would evaporate.

It was a nasty case and it should never have reached the public courts. In Rabbi Zweck's mind it was nasty because it involved Jews, and Jews had their own court, only round the corner from his shop, and it should have been settled there without all the publicity it gathered when it came into the open. A nasty case it was, because it was a family quarrel and they should have been ashamed to let it out of the home. But they were bitter people, the Steinbergs, and they had quarrelled amongst themselves as long as anyone in the district could remember. They had been married for thirty miserable years, the last ten of which had been made even more wretched by the presence of old Mrs Cass, Mrs Steinberg's mother. Of these ten years, Mrs Cass had spent five in bed, stubbornly immortal. Every morning the long suffering Mr Steinberg would take her her tea, and was at pains to hide his disappointment that she was waiting for it. And not only waiting, but grumbling that it was late, that it had too little or too much sugar, that no one cared about her, that she knew she was a lot of trouble, but what was she to do.

'Die,' Mr Steinberg muttered to himself as he left the room. He would join his wife in the kitchen and they would listen to the old woman shouting from the downstairs bedroom, 'You're waiting for me to die, aren't you?'

'Yes, we are,' the Steinbergs muttered separately to themselves, but occasionally Mr Steinberg would speak the thought aloud, and his wife would bombard him with accusations of meanness, inhumanity, and general no-goodness. Their quarrels and the old woman's screaming could be heard intermittently throughout the day and night across the back yards of the neighbourhood, and they had come to be accepted as part of the natural discords of the area.

To complicate matters, there was Mrs Steinberg's brother, a low-life if ever there was one, called Bertie. Bertie's adult life had been punctuated by a series of sudden and prolonged absences, spells in gaol, rushed visits abroad, and periods of lying low. He was a compulsive thief, stealing from friends, strangers and family alike. Mrs Steinberg hated him for the apologies and lies she had to tell on his behalf, for the face she had to keep in front of her friends, although they knew her face-saving tactics and pitied her for them. And she hated her brother because of their pity.

He rarely came to the house to see his mother, for which Mrs Steinberg was on the one hand grateful, but on the other, outraged by his unfilial behaviour. On the rare occasions that he visited, he would pick a quarrel with the old lady, and leave with a piece of silver or anything he could lay his hands on quicker than his sister could remove it, and after each of his departures, Mrs Steinberg would take a belated inventory. And as she viewed her slowly depleting silver collection, she felt grateful that her brother did not come more often.

And then one day, for the first time, she had notice of his coming. Or at least, she fully expected him to show up, as any son, filial or otherwise, would show up to his mother's death bed. For old Mrs Cass had finally made it; after years of threats and curses she had uttered her last. Mrs Steinberg closed her mother's eyes, and guilt-riddled and sob-shaken, she went about the house, clearing the decks.

When Bertie arrived, Mr Steinberg was sitting with the old lady, and when Bertie entered the room, Mr Steinberg left discreetly, suspecting that Bertie had his own private atonements to make. He joined his wife in the kitchen where they sat and stared at each other. Even old Mrs Cass's death had done nothing to soften the loathing between them. If anything it had intensified it, each blaming the other for her passing. 'Don't know what *you're* crying for,' Mrs Steinberg said. 'It's what you've been waiting for, isn't it?'

'Ach,' he spat at her, 'shut your big mouth. Weep, weep,' he went on, 'you got plenty to cry for.'

They heard slow footsteps in the hall, and the slamming of the front door. They looked at each other sharply and it would be fair to suppose that the same question flashed through both their minds. What, besides the body, was takeable in the old lady's room.

They darted to the bedroom, hesitating with respect, in case respect were still in order, at the door. Then, stealthily, they crept inside. She lay there, not surprisingly, as Mr Steinberg had left her, and without moving, he and his wife shot glances about the room, looking for reasons for Bertie's hasty departure. And there it was, or wasn't, as the case may be, and both of them saw it at the same time. The large white no-longer-thereness on the old lady's fourth finger.

'It was there when I left her,' Mr Steinberg whispered, hastening to absolve himself from suspicion.

'Who else, who else?' Mrs Steinberg screamed, careless of her company, 'who else, who else, but Bertie.'

They approached the body, and Mr Steinberg, with the temerity allowed to the next-but-one-of-kin, lifted the naked finger. There it wasn't indeed, neither in the folds of the sheet, nor under the pillow, nor anywhere in the vicinity of the bed. It was gone; the sum total of the old lady's wealth, her inheritance from her husband, his few shares, her pension, her furniture, her silver, all in that giant diamond amalgam that had sat so smugly on her fourth finger. Pogrom money, she used to call it, because it was portable and currency anywhere. But now it was gone, and probably melted down again into cash, and running through Bertie's fingers.

Mrs Steinberg bristled with rage. She would get it back, or at least the value of it, 'if it's the last thing I do,' she shouted. 'Poor Momma,' she whispered, though pity for that quarter was now irrelevant, but it helped to excuse her feelings of unnatural hatred towards her brother.

And so it was, when the old lady was decently buried, and Bertie protesting his innocence on the way to and from the funeral, and all through the *shiva*, that the matter was eventually brought to the courts, and Norman, Rabbi Zweck's boy – a genius he is – was hired to put Mrs Steinberg's case.

The court was crowded. Rabbi Zweck sat at the back in an agony of anxiety. He didn't care too much which way the case went. With Bertie's record, it was a foregone conclusion that he was guilty and he didn't care too much what happened to him. It was Norman and the fear for his performance, that frightened him. He sat with Bella, and she shared his fear, because at that time, two years ago, only they had shared the secret of Norman's drug addiction. They had tried to dissuade him from taking the case, using all kinds of excuses, that he should not get himself mixed up in such a nasty business. They knew his career in Law was finished, but this he would never accept. They were persecuting him, all of them, he said, they refused him his dignity, they were mad.

Why only that morning, before leaving for the courts, he had sprayed the whole flat with insecticide, and thrown his pillows into the bath to drown their evil habitation. He looked yellow and drawn and they had tried again to dissuade him, to give up the case, to send a message to the court that he was not well. 'You're ruining my career,' he shouted at them. 'You want to destroy me completely.' And he had grabbed his gown and briefcase, and made for the door. 'You used to be so proud of me,' he said. 'What happened to you?'

And so he went, to make a public spectacle of himself, so that everyone would know and whisper, 'His great brain is too heavy for him, his genius has driven him mad.' That after all, was the best that Rabbi Zweck could hope for. That people would think that it was Norman's mind that had so shaken him. Not the drugs. Nothing like that. Not the drugs. Even insanity, when closely investigated, allowed for a certain threshold of acceptability. To be driven mad by one's own genius, that was something, that was respectable, an inverted *nachus* almost. But from drugs, that was unpardonable, that was another matter altogether. So Rabbi Zweck and Bella had followed him to court.

They sat in the back row, not because they wanted a quick getaway – they were both prepared to sit it through, whatever the outcome – but because, at the back, they felt more protected, less vulnerable. Around them in the court, their neighbourhood had gathered, transplanted from the area in a body. Most of them secretly hoped for Bertie's acquittal, not because they thought him innocent but because they wanted to punish Mrs

Steinberg, for bringing the matter into the public eye. Jews couldn't be too careful, and it was only asking for trouble if you brought such a squalid exchange into the open. But whatever the outcome, they would be treated to a drama, and to the sight of their home-spun genius – Norman Zweck – thirteen languages he spoke so it was said, Norman the boy who'd made good, of whom, since his infancy, they'd heard so much. It was an outing that the neighbourhood had looked forward to for weeks.

Rabbi Zweck's eyes wandered furtively around the court. He noticed how the women had dressed themselves, and on a week-day too. 'A *Yomtov* they make of it,' he said to himself. Some *Yomtov*. He watched Norman take his seat, and inwardly prayed for him. He disregarded the preliminary paraphernalia of the court proceedings, resting his head on his chest, willing that it would all soon be over. He heard a sudden silence, and then a shuffling of seats, and then his son's voice, stating in cold and somewhat contemptuous tones, the matter of the dispute between the two parties. There was silence as he spoke, broken only by the occasional smacking of lips from the gallery, in anticipation of the treat that was to come. Norman's delivery was lucid and controlled, so much so, that as he progressed with his speech, Rabbi Zweck was able to relax. Bella pressed his arm with her own sense of relief. 'It's all right,' she whispered, 'he's doing very well.' Rabbi Zweck looked around the court. He felt safe enough even to display his pride publicly. He smiled at one or two of his neighbours, acknowledging their nods of congratulation. He felt suddenly well-disposed towards them, and was glad that they had dressed up for the occasion. Norman was going to make it worth their while. His Norman. His clever son, Norman. Doesn't matter what that Dr Levy said. Maybe Norman was right, after all. Dr Levy was only trying to frighten him when he said Norman was slowly committing suicide. Apart from the sleeplessness, Norman was carrying on with his job. Norman was right. He kept saying the pills were good for him. They made him articulate and worthy of respect. He would tell Dr Levy himself. Pity he wasn't in the court to see his son. 'These psychiatrists,' Rabbi Zweck muttered to himself, '*meshuggana*, all of them.'

He heard Mrs Steinberg's name being called, and watched

her as she stepped on to the stand. Mrs Steinberg had not dressed for the occasion. She wore a work-a-day hat and coat and clutched a well-worn leather hold-all that she normally used for her shopping. Norman had probably had a hand in her attire. The magistrate would be more impressed by a simply-dressed hard-working woman, whose sole concern in the case was for justice and not for gain. She took the oath and waited nervously for Norman to begin.

'Mrs Steinberg,' he said, 'would you tell the court in your own words what happened on the morning of Tuesday, 30 April?'

Mrs Steinberg cupped her lips with her hands. 'It all started before then, you know it did,' she hissed at him, hoping that only he would hear.

Norman ignored her plea. 'Mrs Steinberg,' he repeated, 'take your time and tell us the whole story. Let us begin when your mother passed away.'

'But it not the beginning at all,' she hissed again. 'Let me tell them everything.' She dropped her hands to her sides. 'What for do I pay you?' she shouted. 'So you should hide the story of my good-for-nothing brother, the *ganuf* he is. All his life a *ganuf*. Let them know,' she shouted sweeping her arms over her public.

The gallery warmed to her audibly so that the magistrate had to call for silence. 'Would the witness confine herself to answering Counsel's questions,' he said.

Mrs Steinberg turned to the magistrate helplessly. 'The wrong questions he asks,' she pleaded.

'Proceed.' The magistrate nodded at Norman with undeniable authority.

'Mrs Steinberg,' Norman tried again, 'would you tell the court what happened the day your mother died.'

Mrs Steinberg sighed heavily. To start in the middle was no easy task. But she rallied. 'Well,' she said, drawing breath, 'my mother, *olav hashalom*, a very sick woman she was. I should know.' She leaned forward confidentially. 'Ten years I looked after her, up and down, up and down, to and fro, to and fro,' she amended, remembering her mother's downstairs bedroom. 'Everything she wanted, she gets. She wants wireless, she gets;

69

she wants televiscious, she gets; she wants hot water-bottle, she gets. Everything she gets. Should *I* deny her?'

Mrs Steinberg paused while the gallery settled in for her story. Most of them had heard it many times before, but in the market or around her kitchen table, but there was always the possibility of ornamentation with a change of venue.

'Well,' Mrs Steinberg continued, 'my poor mother, she doesn't get any better and . . .'

'Would the witness come to the point?' the magistrate interrupted.

'I'm coming, I'm coming,' she shouted at him. 'All in good time.'

'Where was I?' she said.

'It was the morning of Tuesday, 30 April, the day your mother passed away.' Norman put her back on the rails. 'What happened after your mother died?'

'You want that already?' she said, disappointed.

'What happened after your mother died?' Norman repeated. His voice was gentle and persuasive, so Mrs Steinberg went ahead and told him the whole story.

In the cross-examination that followed, there was little that Bertie's barrister could do to topple Mrs Steinberg's tale, and when Mr Steinberg went into the box it was corroborated in exact detail. It was the first time for many years that the pair had agreed about anything. Their story was unshakeable. Things were going very well for Norman, and Rabbi Zweck by now had lost all his apprehension. He leaned forward to get a better view of his son, regretting that they had had insufficient faith in him to take a seat in the front of the court.

Then it was Bertie's turn in the box, and Norman to cross-examine. Rabbi Zweck watched his son very closely. He felt that Norman was about to show some of the old genius that had singled him out, as a younger man, to be the most brilliant up-and-coming barrister of his time. His son, his clever son, Norman.

'Why did you leave the house so quickly?' Norman was saying.

'I was overcome.' It was a word Bertie had used often during the proceedings. He clearly liked it, though it sat ill-at-ease on him, rough as he was, and apparently without any great sensitivity. 'I was overcome,' he said again. 'I wanted to get away from there. I couldn't stand it any longer.'

'You were overcome,' Norman echoed. 'You were overcome with guilt, perhaps?'

'Perhaps,' Bertie said. He sensed that it was a leading question and he didn't want to commit himself one way or the other.

'What would you have felt guilty about?' Norman said.

Bertie stared at him.

'Perhaps,' Norman helped him along, 'you felt guilty that over the last few years, you had spent very little time with your mother?'

'I saw her,' Bertie mumbled, 'I saw her from time to time.'

'How often in the last year did you visit her?' Norman pursued.

Bertie drummed his fingers on the rail. Every visit was recallable, since each one was associated with some crisis or another. When he'd wanted money, or when he'd wanted to look for her will, or simply to grab what he could from his sister's home. He counted out his visits in terms of loot. There was the silver candlestick, a watch, a camera, and an electric clock. Must get rid of that clock. It was still under his bed in his room. Well, that made at least four visits. He could safely add a couple in which he'd had to cut his losses.

'Half a dozen times,' he said airily.

'That makes once every two months,' Norman said. 'Over the last year, your mother was very ill. Dying, in fact. Would you not say, that in view of the circumstances, your visits were highly infrequent?'

Bertie shrugged his shoulders.

'Did you perhaps live too far away from your mother that a long journey would have been of considerable inconvenience?'

'Huh,' Mrs Steinberg sneered from her seat. 'A stone's throw he lives,' she contributed.

The magistrate silenced her, but she had made her point.

'Where in fact *do* you live?' Norman asked. He wanted it from Bertie's own mouth.

'In Flood Street.'

'How far would you say that was from your sister's home, where your mother lay dying?'

'Five minutes?' Bertie questioned.

'Are you saying five minutes on foot, or five minutes by public transport?' Norman asked, who knew very well where Flood Street was.

'On foot,' Bertie said limply.

'Then it was no great inconvenience for you to visit your dying mother because of the matter of distance,' Norman concluded. 'Then perhaps,' he went on, 'you were prevented from visiting her by your employment?'

'Huh,' Mrs Steinberg couldn't resist it. 'Employment,' she sneered, 'a low good-for-nothing *lobbos*. Who should employ him? Huh,' she added.

The magistrate knocked his knuckles impatiently on the bench. 'I have to warn your client,' he said, addressing himself to Norman, that any further interruptions will result in an adjournment of the case.

'Shush,' Mr Steinberg nudged his wife. Norman looked over to his client reprovingly, then continued with his examination.

'Where are you employed, Mr Cass?'

'I'm unemployed at the moment,' Bertie said.

'And how long have you been unemployed?'

'On and off for about three years.'

'So,' Norman went on hurriedly, 'at the time of your mother's illness, you were not prevented by distance or employment from visiting her.'

Bertie was silent, and Norman allowed the pause.

'Would you call yourself a good son, Mr Cass?' Norman looked over at Mrs Steinberg and was just in time to see her husband clap his hand over her mouth. He smiled in gratitude to Mr Steinberg for giving him the freedom of the floor.

'Well, I loved her,' Bertie said simply.

'But not enough to spend time with her apparently,' Norman said.

Again Bertie was silent, while his counsel fidgeted. Rabbi Zweck relaxed again. Norman had the situation well in hand.

'Tell me in your own words,' Norman said, 'what happened on your last visit to your mother. When she had already passed away.'

'Well,' Bertie began, 'my sister sent a message she had gone. I ran round there and into her room. She was lying on the bed. She . . . *she* was dead. I went and sat by the bed and I looked at her.' He paused. 'And I was overcome,' he added hastily.

'Where were her hands as she lay there?' Norman asked.

'On the sheet, lying by her side.'

'So in your position, sitting by the bed, you were able to see her hands very clearly.'

'Yes, that's right.'

'Describe them to me.'

'Well, they were a bit blue, and there were veins sticking out on them, and they looked very old, and . . . well . . . they were just like . . . hands. Just hands. And oh, there was red polish on the nails. Chipped a bit. It made me feel sort of sick.'

'And the fingers?' Norman asked.

'Well . . . they were . . . just ordinary fingers.'

'Anything on them,' Norman threw off casually.

'No,' Bertie rapped out. 'Nothing at all.'

'Nothing at all?' Norman whispered.

Something in his voice, the sudden quiet, the sudden fear, caused Rabbi Zweck to tighten his stomach. He saw with pain the look on his son's face. It was a look that he knew well, a look that sweated out of his face, oozing from every pore. The silver-fish look that consorted hand in glove with the hallucination.

'Nothing at all?' Norman threatened. He leaned forward, his hands thrown out in a gesture of despair. 'There was a ring,' he thundered.

'It wasn't there,' Bertie said, drawing back and looking round the court for confirmation of his own sense of foreboding.

Norman darted towards him, his face only a hair's breadth from the witness. 'It wasn't there?' he screamed.

The public leaned forward, the magistrate too, a bewildered look crossing his face, not knowing whether to ascribe Norman's outburst to derangement or mere histrionics. A murmur went through the gallery, and Bella, fearing the outcome of it all, clutched her father's arm, not daring to look at him, but knowing that his eyes were glazed with tears, fixed there by fear and a foretaste of disaster.

Bertie backed away as far as he could in the stand. He looked at the magistrate for guidance, but none was forthcoming. He had heard rumours of Norman's behaviour. Norman was a whispered word in the neighbourhood, probably because of his genius, a whisper that was a stifled reference to something that was not quite understood. But madness or genius, both were baitable. 'No,' he said defiantly, 'like I said, it wasn't there.'

Norman shook his head, unbelieving. He dropped his hands to his sides, and shrunk backwards to his stand. Rabbi Zweck watched him sadly. He knew that helpless gesture, that unfailing response to, 'They're not there. It's your imagination.' Bertie's denial had been for Norman a personal affront. For the last two years, his waking hours had been punctuated by just that kind of smug assertion. 'It's not there, it's not there.'

'Of course it was there,' Rabbi Zweck muttered. 'You know, Bertie Cass, you know bloody well it was there. Tell him, tell him,' he pleaded, 'tell my son it was there.'

Norman folded his arms. His body seemed to relax. He even smiled a little. The audience and the presiding magistrate were relieved. His outburst had obviously been tactical; he had tried to threaten Bertie into admission. Now, that line having failed, he was about to try another. But Rabbi Zweck and Bella felt no such relief. Norman's smile was frighteningly familiar. They knew it as a prelude to argument, to his patient insistence that all were mad and only he was sane. They clutched each other's hands.

'Well, Mr Cass,' Norman said politely, 'you say that it wasn't there. Good enough. Now tell me, Mr Cass, how long had your mother been dead when you came to see her?'

Bertie did not see the relevance of the question, but he could find no threat in it. 'I don't know,' he said amicably. He was grateful for Norman's friendly tone. 'I came as soon as I was called. So perhaps she had been dead for about an hour.'

'Good enough,' Norman said. 'Very shortly after death, as you know full well, Mr Cass, a rot sets into the body. You would agree with that?'

'I don't know,' Bertie said. He was not altogether happy with Norman's respectful tone. 'I don't know anything about those things.'

'Well, that is so, Mr Cass. It is a fact that could be confirmed by any pathologist.'

The audience leaned forward curious about the purpose of Norman's discourse. They expected a trap, and marvelled at its gentlemanly laying.

'Did you see any worms on your mother?' Norman's arms were still folded, and his smile was ingratiating.

'No, of course not,' Bertie said, offended by his bad taste.

'Your mother was dead long enough for worms,' Norman said. 'But you didn't see them.'

'No,' Bertie said again.

'I understand that you didn't see them,' Norman said generously. 'You were too overcome. You were in a state of acute distress. Yet you can take my word for it, Mr Cass, the worms were there all right, and it was quite natural in your state of shock that you didn't see them.'

Bertie nodded dubiously.

'So you would agree,' Norman went on, 'that certain things can be present, yet you cannot see them, especially if you are in a state of shock.'

Bertie kept his mouth firmly shut.

'Therefore,' Norman went on, 'there might well have been a ring on your late mother's finger, and you, in your state of profound despair, didn't see it.'

'If I didn't see it,' Bertie said without hesitation, 'then I couldn't have taken it, could I?' He sighed with his triumph.

'Exactly,' Norman said. 'You most certainly couldn't have taken it, if you couldn't see it, whether it was there or not.'

'I am not quite clear where this line of questioning is leading,' the magistrate said.

'I hope to make myself clear very shortly.'

There was nothing disturbing or untoward in Norman's manner. He was relaxed still, and smiling, and even Rabbi Zweck thought for a moment that he had been misled. Yet it did appear that Norman's line of questioning indicated that he was changing sides.

'So you didn't see it, Mr Cass,' Norman was saying. 'Yet we know that a ring was present and that it was taken. Therefore we must assume, must we not, that it was taken by someone who was able to see it.'

Bertie nodded, bewildered.

'We have from Mrs Steinberg's testimony, and Mr Steinberg's too, for that matter, that a ring was on your late mother's finger and was positively seen by both of them. We have no evidence that anyone else saw the ring. And we know that the ring could only have been taken by someone who saw it.'

A murmur went round the court. Mrs Steinberg opened her mouth to speak, but nothing came out. She shoved her husband in horror, and he shoved her back, regretting their earlier collaboration.

Norman unfolded his arms, and left his stand. He walked towards the magistrates bench. 'Your Honour,' he said. 'I am in no way accusing my own clients of theft as you may have supposed from my line of argument. But I will have no truck with people who refuse to see things.'

The magistrate leaned forward. He hadn't the faintest idea of what Norman was about. Norman had shown no ignorance of the case, nor a lack of preparation, otherwise he could have adjourned the court, and advised the plaintiffs to find themselves another lawyer. There had been such simple and irrefutable logic in Norman's argument, and his manner had been so self-assured and calm, that he wondered on what basis he could call for an adjournment.

'There are too many people in this world,' Norman was saying, 'who refuse to admit that things are there, who say, "No, I cannot see them, they're in your imagination." We all know,' he went on patiently, and turning to the body of the court, 'that certain things exist, and their existence is denied by certain people for their own motives in order to drive other people mad. Your Honour,' he turned to the Bench again, 'I want nothing to do with that type of person. I submit that Bertie Cass is not a thief. He is a lunatic and he should be put away.' He tugged at his gown on his shoulder and walked back to his stand.

The magistrate coughed to hide his own bewilderment. 'I

move the case be adjourned,' he said, wiping the sweat that had already gathered on his forehead. He indicated to his clerk that Norman should come to his chambers, and he left the court.

Norman waited for the court to empty. Only his father and Bella remained. He had sat down, his body hunched over the desk. With his black gown streaking the floor, he looked like a fallen blackbird. Rabbi Zweck went up to him. 'Come home, Norman,' he said. 'Is overstrain. A rest you need.'

For some reason, Norman offered no resistance. He took his father's hand like a child, and Bella followed them. At the door, he turned round and looked sadly at the empty chamber, as if even he had to admit to himself that he could never enter it again.

Rabbi Zweck mopped the sweat from his cheeks and beard. He noticed that Mrs Golden was crying. She too, had come to the end of the recollection, though how long ago, Rabbi Zweck could not guess. He had laboured alone into the past, oblivious of his present company. He watched as she wiped her eyes on the cuff of her coat sleeve. 'But is all over now,' he said, trying to introduce a little cheer into his voice. 'Much better he is. They told me is getting better.'

Mrs Golden sniffled. 'You should only have joy from him,' she said.

'Joy,' Rabbi Zweck echoed. 'I'll do without the joy. He should only be well.'

It was only when Mrs Golden had left the shop that Rabbi Zweck realized what he had offered to forego from his son. Did not every father have the right to expect *nacchus* from his children. 'Rights, rights,' Rabbi Zweck muttered to himself. 'Who should have rights. So long he gets better. Nothing else. Just better he should get. Such a right he should have, my son Norman should have.'

He stood at the counter, hanging on with his fists to his lapels, and shaking to and fro in an attitude of prayer. 'I give up my rights,' he said, 'I give them up.'

As he rung up Mrs Golden's order in the till, he paused with one finger on the key. 'Too late it is, already,' he muttered.

8

Bella found herself in Norman's room. She had come there out of habit, as she came every morning, nagging him to get out of bed, to pull himself together, to stop his nonsense, and do you get pleasure out of driving us both mad. Look what you're doing to your father. In the end, it will kill him. It had been her matins for the last five years during each bout of Norman's illness.

Now she missed him. It was ridiculous, but she missed him. And she had to admit, she missed him for her own sake. Now there was no one to punish, no one to diminish, no target for her own bitter feelings of inadequacy. For a moment she wished him back, lying there, yellow with a sleepless night, the floor sprinkled with insecticide, and the mirror covered to hide the echo of his horrible imaginings. Yes, she wished him back. He had become a necessity for her, the sick Norman, the failed Norman, the scapegoat for all her unhappiness. Listlessly, she picked up the papers that her father had left on the bed the previous night. She stuffed them back into a drawer. She wanted no part in the discovery of his source of supply. It was pointless. An addict could replace one source with another, with a speed and efficiency in direct ratio to his needs. She shut all the half-open drawers and looked around the room. It was tidy now, the bed changed, and the windows open with fresh air. It had taken Bella a half an hour to erase Norman from the room, and she wished for a moment that she had left it as it was, with all the visible signs of his madness. She sat on the bed, and noticed with a smile that her feet did not touch the floor. She remembered how, before her mother had died, she could sit on the bed, and without even stretching her legs, she could follow with her toes, the fading rose pattern of the carpet. It was just that since her mother had died, the bed was higher, that much higher by two eiderdowns, one belonging to her mother, and the other to her sister Esther. She had noticed the same sudden sproutings in other bedrooms of the neighbourhood, how with each death and each departure, beds seemed to grow higher, and that it was no reflection on your height or lack of it, if you could not touch the ground from off a Jewish bed.

She looked down at her dangling feet. A varicose vein burst out from underneath her white ankle-sock. Only a children's playground or a tennis court could have legitimized those white socks, not a mad brother's bedroom on a double-decker bed. She remembered how she first started to wear them, as a little girl almost forty years ago, the excitement of turning down the bright white top, and lovingly pressing it into a neat fold. How she had folded one first, then lined her feet together, to get the exact fold on the other foot. Now she found no joy in turning them down; she had lost all interest in their symmetry. But she could not stop wearing them. Every day, a clean pair, from the dozens of pairs in her drawer, and every day, the inability to discard them. She recalled her first rebellion against the white socks, the first, and indeed the last stand she took against her mother's endless perpetuation of her daughter's childhood. It was Norman's sixteenth birthday, the morning of his bar-mitzvah. A belated one, three years belated, according to the Jewish Law, but behind the delay lay a story that possibly held the seeds of Norman's present torment. But how could anyone know, Bella thought, how it had all started? In any case, madness had no precise beginning or end. Norman was in a nut-house, and she was sitting on his bed. For her, his incarceration was probably the end of things. For Norman it was possibly the beginning. There's madness for you. Who knows when it started, she thought. Perhaps in his childhood, in her father's childhood, in her own, even. She looked at her socks and hurriedly tucked her feet under her on the bed. Madness started or it finished, she decided, whichever way you chose to look at it, according to the nature of your own problem. And so she recalled the story, because she needed to, because she needed to acknowledge her part in her brother's disintegration.

Norman was five years old, and she a year his junior. He had picked up a young Polish boy, who had drifted into the neigh-bourhood, and after about three months of solid street com-panionship, Norman brought the boy to the house, and they spoke together in fluent Polish. Mrs Zweck, who had long been convinced that there was something special about her first-born, now set about his education in earnest. She sought out a French teacher, 'Is cultured, the French language,' she would say. 'Is nice people the French,' as opposed in her mind to the Poles, whose worldly philosophy, i.e. their attitude to the Jews, was barbaric, and so possibly was their language. So Norman was farmed out to French, the posh tongue, which he mastered with little difficulty by the time he was six. By the age of seven, he was fluent in Polish, French and English, together with Yiddish and Hebrew which he had picked up between times from his parents.

In his ninth year, Mrs Zweck, who had a prophetic blockage on German, finally relented, since 'all knowledge, even the German, is power,' and Norman with a contempt possibly in-herited from his mother, refused to ascribe difficulties or subtle-ties to the tongue, and mastered it with even more speed than the others. 'My son, the linguist,' Mrs Zweck would introduce him. 'Speak a little French,' and then, when this accomplish-ment had been, in one or two sentences, proved, she would make the same requests for each tongue. From all over the country, journalists came, armed with cameras and note-books, and overnight, Norman Zweck became a household word. 'How old is he?' they marvelled.

'Nine,' his proud mother would answer, and it was the last time that she was truthful about her son's age. Subsequently, with each new language Norman acquired, he lost one year, so that, after putting Italian, Spanish and Russian under his hat, he was, in spite of his twelve years, and in all the papers, for the public's memory is short, still only nine years old. 'Only nine yet,' Mrs Zweck would beam. 'Such a son I have.'

Then Norman didn't want any more. He was tired of being the freak in the circus, and he wanted to be twelve, like the other boys in the neighbourhood. Rabbi Zweck saw his point. 'So what's so wrong in knowing nine languages, and being twelve? Is still very clever,' he said. 'Let the boy be his age.'

But Mrs Zweck was adamant. It was too late to retract on her son's primogeniture. He couldn't overnight become three years older. It would give the lie to all her stories over the years. 'I don't care if he doesn't want more language, a lazy good-for-nothing he is, if I say he's nine, he's nine, next year, God willing, he will be ten, and so on, and so on, he should have a long life. Plenty of time to put on your age.'

'And what about Bella?' Rabbi Zweck said.

'Bella is eight,' Mrs Zweck said, with finality.

'She's eleven,' Rabbi Zweck said, with utmost honesty, 'and she won't thank you for it.'

'You want she should be older than Norman, when everyone knows a boy is our first-born.'

Rabbi Zweck was silent. She was hard to budge, and he understood why. She had to maintain the illusion she had created, for the sake of her own reputation. 'What about the barmitzvah?' he ventured. 'We cannot deceive *Ha Shem*.'

'He will understand,' she said with confidence. 'So long we make a barmitzvah, what difference when?'

'I don't like it,' Rabbi Zweck said.

'You want I should look a fool?' she shouted at him. 'With all those stories of him in the papers?'

It was the end of the argument. In spite of his intermittent protestations, and Norman's stubborn retirement from his studies, his thirteenth birthday passed heretically by. And on his sixteenth birthday, more than bristling on his chin, he was allowed to make his Covenant with the Lord.

Breakfast was late and in snatches in the flat that morning. Mrs Zweck was trying to dress Esther, the youngest, seven years old in anyone's terms, the spoilt Esther, untouched by her mother's arithmetic. Then Mrs Zweck had to organize herself and put the finishing touches to the prepared cold lunch. She adjusted the hat she'd had made for the occasion, and joined the others in the kitchen. Mrs Zweck patted Norman on the head, though he was a good deal taller than his mother. 'So today, you make it,' she said proudly. 'A man, you'll be. My son, a linguist' – the apposition was a habit with her – 'is a man already.'

'I've been a man for three years,' he hissed. 'Who's kidding whom?'

'Shush,' Rabbi Zweck said. He didn't want any argument. 'Let's go already. Is late.'

Bella, whose legs had been hidden under the table, moved towards the door.

'Oi veh,' moaned Mrs Zweck, 'what is it on your legs?'

'Stockings,' Bella said, trembling. 'Silk stockings from your drawer.'

Mrs Zweck gaped.

'I'm fifteen,' Bella reminded her.

'You're twelve,' Mrs Zweck shouted. 'You hear? You're twelve. Next year, please God, you are thirteen. Go put on the socks. At your age in stockings. Plenty time to be grown up. Believe me. Go change,' she screamed at her.

Bella stood her ground, terrified.

'Bella,' Rabbi Zweck said gently, 'what difference after all?'

'No,' Bella said. 'If I can't wear stockings, I'm not going.'

'You'll change. You hear me?' Mrs Zweck thundered.

'No.'

The slap came almost as she said it, and another slap, and another, as Mrs Zweck saw her fantasy, carefully woven over the years, dismissed so flagrantly by one of her own flesh and blood.

'Go Bella, go change,' said her father. 'You see how it upsets Momma. Bellale,' he pleaded, 'for your mother, go change.'

She stood in the doorway, hesitant, but long enough to hear Norman say, 'For Christ's sake, Bella, go and put on your socks.'

Bella and her stockings were at once forgotten, an oh so minor misdemeanour in the face of her brother's outrageous blasphemy.

'Never before in my house,' Rabbi Zweck whispered.

'And on his barmitzvah day,' Mrs Zweck echoed.

Rabbi Zweck stood and raised his hand to his son. 'Take it back,' he thundered. 'Such words in my house. I should live.'

Mrs Zweck stayed his hand in the air. 'Say you're sorry Norman. Say quick you're sorry. Quick, quick,' she panicked.

'I'm sorry,' Norman said, and Bella heard him repeat it at his mother's demand, again and again, as if to exorcise the word. She reached the bedroom. They had enough on their hands. She couldn't expect them to take on her stockings too. Meekly she took them off, and followed, white hosed, to the synagogue.

Bella shifted her feet from under her, and dangled them once more over Norman's bed. She couldn't recollect the events in the synagogue. That part of the story must have been irrelevant to her need. So it was the home-coming that crept into her mind, though she consciously tried to turn it away. In it was perhaps the beginnings of her brother's anguish, and possibly her own. She lay back on Norman's bed, and fully outstretched, she willed herself to experience again the event that followed her brother's barmitzvah.

She had come back to the flat, first, and alone, to make the final preparations for the lunch party. There was little to do, and she was glad to go to her room and be alone. She left her door open, so that she could hear them coming up the stairs to the flat. She sat on the bed, but in that position, she could not avoid the sight of the white flags of surrender on her feet. So she lay down, flat, so that they could not offend her. She wondered when she would be allowed, even encouraged, to give them up, and whether she ever would. After her small rebellion that morning and all through the ceremony, she had begun to feel that the white socks had taken over, that they had become more than just a symbol of the lie of years; they had stunted her growth for ever.

She heard a quick movement of footsteps up the stairs, two at a time, in a hurry, then the opening of the front door. She waited, not understanding her excitement. He came straight to her room. He shut the door behind him, his back towards it, and his hand behind the back, still on the handle.

'Where are the others?' Bella said.

'They'll be ages,' Norman answered her. 'I left them yakking outside *shul*. They'll be ages,' he repeated.

She didn't look at him. She knew and expected something to happen.

Something had to happen between them. Two people cannot

play a conspiracy for so long, and play it each on his own. There came a moment, when, in the dross of lies, the truth, known to them both, had to be asserted, and for their own sanity, shared.

He came over towards the bed. 'After tomorrow, when all the fuss is over,' he said, 'I'm going to be sixteen, whatever anyone says, and you can take off those socks.'

She looked at him, and was glad that he was smiling at her.

'Well,' he said, 'shove over.' He chose the word to hide his embarrassment. He laughed a little too, in order to ridicule what he intuitively knew was going to be desperately important to both of them.

'Draw the curtains,' Bella said.

Norman went over to the window, and as he did so, Bella slipped inside the sheets. Now the room was quite dark, and she felt her brother moving beside the bed, and soon, his forbidden body alongside her.

Rabbi and Mrs Zweck led the way from the synagogue, little Esther tugging behind. 'What a performance, our Norman,' Mrs Zweck said, licking her lips. She patted Rabbi Zweck's hand. 'I was proud. A good son we have.'

'Bella, too,' Rabbi Zweck said. He paused. 'Sarahle, forget already the socks. Is not right for a big girl like Bella.'

Mrs Zweck stopped in her tracks. 'Who wants with socks any more. After tomorrow, no more socks. She should grow up already. Looking at the boys she should be. Is funny, Abie,' she confided, 'but no interest she seems to have with the boys. Look today, how she runs home. Did I tell her to go. Everything's ready. No she's got to run. Nice boys in *shul* today. All nice boys. What for she's running away?'

'Is the socks,' Rabbi Zweck said.

'So finish with the socks,' Mrs Zweck almost shouted, as if she'd had no hand in their beginning. 'Finish with the socks, and we should both live to dance at her wedding.'

Meanwhile the guests had caught up with them, and taking up the whole pavement in four serried ranks, they returned in festive mood to the flat. Mrs Zweck opened the door with her key, and led the guests into the dining-room. Everything was ready. Bella was standing at the table, ready to serve. Mrs Zweck noticed a flush on her cheek, and attributed it to her shyness and excitement of the occasion. Norman stood at the other end of the room, a little pale, his mother thought, but also, God bless him, because of the excitement. Something in his look prompted Mrs Zweck to look again at Bella. She stood as before, flushed a little, and waiting. Mrs Zweck looked back at Norman, then again at Bella, as if something in each of them magnetically bounced off the other, like a ball that moved between two players without their participation. Whatever it was, Mrs Zweck sensed that she was excluded from it, and standing between them, looking involuntarily from one to the other, she wondered why she felt suddenly disturbed.

Bella sat up on Norman's bed, and looked at her socks. Norman had indeed become sixteen on the following day, and without any difficulty. But she had found it hard to assume her natural age. Besides, the socks were not so easily discarded. She didn't know why she couldn't relinquish them. Perhaps she had wanted to maintain her mother's illusion, even though her brother had opted out of the play, and she could not find it in herself to let her mother down. She bent over the bed to tidy the fold in her sock. In her heart she knew why she would not let them go. They were all she had to perpetuate her brother's love. Had she allowed herself womanhood, their coupling would have been meaningless.

'So what?' she said aloud and stood up. Her mother was dead; she owed no more to that quarter, and Norman, well, he was away, and this love of hers for him, it had to stop, it had to stop, it was crippling both of them. What had she done with her life after all, forever justifying her infant extremities? She had settled for sterility, and called it maturity. She ran to her room and opened the spare drawer. When Esther had left home she had left, among other things, a pair of stockings, or, it crossed Bella's mind, had she left them deliberately? It didn't really matter what Esther's motives were. Esther was doing her no favours. This was her own decision. She tore the cellophane bag and gently took out the stockings and laid them on the bed. For a moment she stared at them, trying to see them as a natural part of herself, as the white socks had always been. It was difficult. But she would get used to them. She would have to. She tore off one sock, and sat down on the bed. Slowly she drew on the stocking, with a stab of despair at the thought of a sock-less future. Like Norman she had become an addict, and white was the colour of her illusion as well. But she would be stronger than Norman. She would will herself into a cure. With her stockinged foot, she eased off the other sock and as it fell to the floor, the telephone rang. She waited, listening to its ring, sitting there on the bed, her bare and stockinged feet dangling. She knew it was Norman. Something had warned him of the change at home. Something had told him that Bella was in the process of discarding him. She ran to the phone, the one stocking concertinaed to her ankle.

'Hullo.'

'Bella?'

'How are you?'

'I'm fine, fine. I'm much better. This place is wonderful. It's doing me a lot of good already.' He was breathless with rehearsal.

'I'm glad, glad,' Bella said. Her voice was automatic, and she was shocked at herself that the news did not gladden her. She hoped that her lack of enthusiasm hadn't spread into her voice. 'That's marvellous,' she said tonelessly. 'What are they doing to you?'

'It's sleep. I had a wonderful sleep last night, and they're giving me tranquillizing pills.'

There followed an uneasy silence.

'D'you want me to come and see you?' she asked tentatively.

'Yes. I thought you might come up today. It's half day in the shop. I thought you might come with Poppa.'

'Well, one of us will come anyway.' She was glad that she had a let-out. She didn't want to see him, and had to reluctantly admit to herself that the thought of his getting better, disturbed her. 'D'you want anything?' she asked.

'Yes,' Norman said hurriedly. 'I need some money. I've got this mad craving for chocolate. Lots and lots of chocolate. And I need to buy shaving soap and lots and lots of toilet things. Just bring the money, and I'll buy the stuff here. We've got a little shop. It's quite a community. But I could do with some chocolate. God, even to talk about it makes my mouth water.'

Bella leaned over the telephone. She felt weak. He was talking like a child, and in a surge of love she would join him in his regression. She bent down and slipped the silk stocking off her foot. 'You'll have chocolate, Norman,' she said gently, 'as much as you want.'

'This afternoon, I want it,' he said impatiently. 'You will come, won't you.'

'We'll be there,' she said. She hesitated before she put the phone down. 'We love you, Norman,' she said. Her father would have to shoulder the blame for that love too. She couldn't bear it alone. They would go and see him together and she in her white socks, because although her mother was dead, and Norman in hospital, and as he said, getting better, between them the illusion was the same.

9

The thought of a shopping spree on Norman's behalf excited her, and she decided to take a bus out of their own squalid shopping area to a district farther into the town, where a greater variety was available. On the bus, Bella listed what she would buy him and when her stop came, she watched some passengers alight, but she didn't join them. She turned away from the window, pretending to herself that she had missed her stop, and when she alighted, three stops later, she tried to convince herself that she'd reached Esther's home by accident. She rarely went to see her sister. Esther was so unhappy that Bella felt it as a punishment to herself. It was more comfortable to keep in touch by letter. But what she had to tell about Norman's confinement was not easily written down. Besides, she wanted the gratification of seeing Esther's reaction. In a way, it would off-load her own burden. She hoped that the husband was at work. She could not bring herself to pronounce his name. She blamed him for her sister's unhappiness, though she knew in her heart that he was innocent, that he'd been used in a marriage that was doomed from the start. But she had to blame somebody, and John had always made himself available for blame. Over the years, he had willingly stood accused. He even blamed himself for not being Jewish, and therefore the cause of the family rift. He offered no hostility, just a quiet and gentle penitence that Bella found quite sickening. She knew that in anyone else's terms, John was a good man, whose only sin lay in loving and continuing to love her sister. It was possibly envy that antagonized her, and this thought made her dislike him more.

She waited in the doorway before ringing the bell. She looked over the neat square of lawn that fronted the house, each blade of grass an exact length, and hand-trimmed at the edges. John's work. The white slatted fence enclosing the lawn was John's work too, an attempt to relieve the privet hedge monotony of the semis along the road. John had tried. Even the *mezzuzah* on the front door was John's work. Esther would never have put it there. She had married out, and she saw no point in any pretence. But John had taken the responsibility on her behalf. He had nailed it to the wrong side of the door. But what did it matter? Inside as well, it was all John's work. Esther had contributed little to the homemaking, as if she had never regarded her union as anything but temporary. Most of her books, and even some of her clothes, were after twenty years still in the flat, and Esther had never asked for them, for their removal would have made the break final. Bella often suggested to her sister that she should visit the flat and take the risk of being turned away. And it *was* a risk, because her father had promised her dying mother that Esther should not be forgiven. No, he would have to die before Esther could come home. Bella shivered at the thought. She had never admitted that eventuality, and she cursed Esther, and wished her from home for ever. She looked forward to breaking the news about Norman. She had to make her suffer a little.

She rang the door bell and waited. She knew she would have to wait for a while. In a house where there are few callers, there is often a long interval between the bell and its acknowledgement. There must be time for reflection on who it might be, for no one is ever expected, then a time for anxiety that the mundane but safe pattern of life had changed, a time to feel fear and uncertainty, and then, in practical terms, time for the hesitant steps to the door. Bella timed each episode, and the door opened.

It was John. 'The Library's closed today,' he said quickly. 'It's the local elections.' He was deeply apologetic for being found in his own home. He smiled weakly. 'I'll get Esther,' he said.

He effaced himself quickly from the doorway and Bella walked inside.

'It's Bella,' she heard John shout. Almost immediately, Esther ran into the hall. Her face was drawn with anxiety. 'Is Poppa all right?' she whispered. 'He's not ill, is he?' She was terrified of Bella's presence. Every knock at the door was a foretaste of the news that for almost twenty years she had dreaded with day to day fear, the news that it was too late for her father's forgiveness. 'Bella,' she whispered again, alarmed by her sister's silence, 'is he all right?'

'He's fine. I was just passing, and I dropped in to see you.'

'I'll make you both some coffee,' they heard John's voice. He would serve them and withdraw himself as the outsider they both claimed him to be.

'You've got something to tell me,' Esther said. 'You've never just dropped in. There's always been some reason. What is it?' she said, sitting down and trying to compose herself. 'It's going to happen to me one day, I know. Is it today, Bella?'

'He's fine,' Bella said, sitting herself on the arm of Esther's chair. She put her arm round her sister. In spite of herself, she was moved by Esther's concern and the thought of all her lonely days and nights punctured with fear for her father. 'There's nothing wrong with Poppa,' Bella said. 'You don't have to worry about him. It's Norman.'

'Silver-fish again? Poor Poppa,' Esther said. 'How can he stand it?'

'It's pretty bad this time,' Bella said shortly. She was angry that Esther saw only her father's suffering, when God knows, it was breaking her too. 'We had to put him away.' She used the term deliberately, to punish Norman for his lunacy and what it was doing to them.

'Is he in a hospital then?' Esther tried to mollify her sister's terminology.

'If that's what you want to call it,' Bella said.

'Poor Bella,' Esther took her sister's hand. 'It's a terrible life for you.'

With this recognition, Bella softened, and patiently, and in detail, she told her story of their brother's latest turning.

'What can I do?' Esther said helplessly when Bella had finished. 'I don't suppose he's allowed visitors?' she asked hopefully. She dreaded that she would have to face him, and him prone and mad to boot, and at every kind of disadvantage. What could his hate or forgiveness mean from such a position. 'I'll wait till he gets better,' she said quickly. 'I'll invite him here.'

'He's allowed visitors,' Bella said coldly. 'I'm going with Poppa to see him this afternoon.'

'Does Poppa have to go? Can't you spare him that?' She saw Bella's hurt face, 'I can't go,' she said quietly. 'I just couldn't face it.'

Bella stood up. 'Don't you *care*?' she screamed at her. 'You only think of yourself. Your brother's ill. He's never been so bad, and all you can think about is something that happened almost twenty years ago, and you're too proud to admit that you were wrong. I know Norman was wrong too,' she said before Esther could interrupt her, 'but why can't you forget it? He needs you,' she said. 'Even you. He needs us all.'

John came into the room with a tray of coffee. Esther was glad of the respite and she smiled at him. His return smile conspired with understanding, and it pained her that he was so good a man, and she, so unworthy. She thought of her suitcases in their bedroom, which since their marriage she had not unpacked, and how each night, he stepped over them to the bed, without a word. She thought of the nursery he had patiently fitted out, and how, over the years, she had turned it into a lumber room. He was a man who would wait in dignity, and who, with equal dignity, was prepared to lose.

He poured the coffee for them, and Bella noticed that he had brought no cup for himself. She wanted him to stay. His presence would relieve the tension between them. Besides, for some reason, she felt a little closer to him. 'Where's your cup, John?' she said.

Esther looked up, startled at the name. Neither was she pleased by Bella's friendly tone. She didn't want an alliance between them. Here was a union that she knew she would eventually break, and she didn't want the complication of allies, either on John's side or her own. 'John doesn't drink coffee,' she said quickly. She touched his arm to offset the abruptness in her voice, and John left them, glad to efface himself.

'Don't involve him Bella,' Esther said. 'It's got nothing to do with him.'

They drank their coffee. 'Will you go and see Norman?' Bella tried again.

'It's Poppa I'm worried about. It can't be good for him, these visits and that awful journey. Bella,' she said, 'ring me every day. Please. You will, won't you. I have to know how he is.'

Bella buttoned her coat. 'D'you want to come shopping with me. Norman asked for chocolate.'

'How you still spoil him,' Esther said, almost to herself. 'All his life. Whatever he wanted. And look at him. A wretched drug addict. I don't care about him,' she said savagely. 'I honestly don't care.'

Bella moved towards the door, and Esther followed her. 'Does Poppa know you came?'

'No,' Bella's voice was cold. 'He never mentions you.'

'Try to talk to him a little about me Bella, please. Just say my name. You only have to do that. Just once. And then once again.' She clutched her sister's arm. 'Don't let him forget me, Bella.'

'I try,' Bella lied. Her sister's name was a forbidden word in the house. Even in childhood recollections it was disallowed. Bella could have tried harder, she knew, but over the years she had refrained. Her father had his pride too.

They reached the front door. 'Say good-bye to John for me,' Bella said.

'Give Poppa my love.'

Bella was silent.

'But you can try, can't you,' she pleaded. 'Just say, Esther sends her love.' She spelt out each word separately. 'Bella,' she whispered, 'don't you *want* me to come home?'

'It's up to Poppa,' Bella said. 'I'll do what I can.' But she had already dismissed Esther's plea. Her father's pride was as stubborn as Esther's but for Bella, it had greater value. He was an old man, and his pride retarded his ageing. If he were to lose it, he would shrivel into ineffectuality. No, if Esther were ever to come home, it would have to be on his authority, an authority she would not trespass.

'Ring me,' Esther said. 'Let me know every day. You will, won't you, Bella.'

Her pleading invested Bella with a sense of her own power, with the awareness that she was within the crisis, within her brother's madness and her father's agony, while Esther would have to tremble at the end of a telephone, ousted from it all. She pitied her, and out of her pity, she kissed her.

'Just speak my name to him,' Esther said again.

10

Bella clutched the parcel of Norman's requests under her arm. She wanted only the best for him, and what kind of collection could he get in the hospital shop? So she had bought him the most exclusive chocolates and toiletries whose price had disgusted her. She had wrapped them all carefully, separately and then together in a parcel tied with pink ribbon. She felt childishly excited, as if she were going to a party with a present. Rabbi Zweck dragged behind her.

It was a long walk from the bus-stop to the hospital, but he was glad of it. It would give him time to collect his thoughts and to rehearse what he would say to his son. Throughout the hour-long journey from London they had sat together in silence, and he had thought about it over and over again. And each time he had postponed the decision as to what he would say. His attention anyway had been distracted. He recalled his previous journey to the hospital, only the day before, yet already it had assumed the unreal quality of a nightmare. He recognized the route that the black car had assaulted, the occasional landmarks, and all had been painful. The tiny 'olde worlde' antique shop in the centre of a passing village had kindled the memory of Norman's final protest against the journey. At the end of the row of houses, he heaved a great sigh of abdication. Rabbi Zweck looked at his fellow passengers on the bus and wondered how they could remain so unaffected by his own torment. He was glad when he and Bella got off, although the last stage of the journey forced him to face the necessity of deciding how he should greet his son.

He kept to the inside of the pavement, walking under the overhanging trees, as if keeping out of everyone's way although, apart from Bella, there was not a soul in sight. At the bus-stop, only they had alighted. The other passengers had saner connections. They were going home, or out to tea, or shopping, none of them on an expedition that involved dishonesty or disguise. 'Hullo, Norman,' Rabbi Zweck whispered to himself. 'How are you?' How should he be, Rabbi Zweck thought, cooped up in that open pen, pecked at by *meshuggana* from all sides. Rabbi Zweck shuddered. 'Hullo, Norman,' he tried again. 'Is hot today.' No, that was no good either. Hot or cold, what difference did it make to a man to whom temperature was no more than a sickly irrelevancy to his hallucinated day. 'Hullo, Norman,' he whispered again. And there he paused. It was the least and also the most that he could say.

They reached the hospital gates. In front of them, at a fork in the path, was a large notice pointing in the directions of the various numbered villas. Bella looked at her father for guidance, but he did not know the number of Norman's hut. Nevertheless, he carried straight on knowing that his steps would take him there involuntarily, and probably by the shortest route.

All the villas looked exactly alike, red-brick structures, aproned by patios and well laid-out gardens. A few groups were scattered on the lawns, family groups they seemed, with children and themos-flasks, with their pyjama-clad member in the middle. Rabbi Zweck's heart turned at the sight of them, at the picture of complete family surrender. There they were, not only accepting their heartache, but making a life of it too. He hoped Norman was in bed, where he ought to be, confined until he was better, and getting out of bed only when he was ready to go straight home. They reached a glass portal and Rabbi Zweck recognized the entrance. Part of the lower wall-facing had crumbled on one side, and he remembered how Norman's hand had grasped at it as he stumbled out of the black car. 'This is the one,' he turned to Bella. The crumbling wall was the only familiarity with the place that he would ever allow himself, and even that he would reject as soon as Norman's stay was over.

Bella followed him up the steps. Through the glass of the tea corridor, a table-tennis table had been set up, and Rabbi Zweck recognized the two players. First it was Norman's back that he knew, darting from side to side with an agility and an abandon that Rabbi Zweck found unnerving. But even more disturbing was the recognition of his son's partner, the man, who the night before, had sat bolt upright in the bed opposite and stared at him. 'We've got to get out of here,' Rabbi Zweck whispered to Bella. '*Meshuggana*, the lot of them, and my son – he enjoys it. A *Yomtov* he makes from it. Come.'

He swung the doors open and strode inside, determined to put an end to all this happiness. Minister saw him first. He caught Norman's return ball in his hand, 'Look who's arrived,' he yelled across the table. 'Your accountant.'

Norman dropped his bat and slowly turned to face them. He stared at them for a while, standing there sheepishly at the door, his father, stooping with shame and pity, and Bella, her arm on his shoulder, protecting him. He felt like a child at a school prize-giving, when his parents arrived and he was thoroughly ashamed of them. But the feeling was immediately followed by one of compassion, and he streched out his arms to welcome them, to put them at their ease, to make them feel at home. 'Come in,' he said gently, as if he had proprietory rights on the place. 'Meet my friends.'

'Friends already,' Rabbi Zweck shivered.

'Yes, my friends,' Norman said, spelling it out, glad that he was able to resume hostilities. 'They're my friends,' he said again. 'We've all got something in common.'

'What's that?' Bella said, because it might as well be out and done with.

'Families,' Minister said. He had crossed over to the other end of the table and he was looking at Bella with crude fascination. 'You 'is mother, then?' he said.

Bella ignored him and handed the parcel out to Norman. 'This is for you,' she said.

Norman hesitated before taking it, fearing what it might contain. 'You've gone and bought up a whole bloody chocolate shop,' he said, furious. He snatched the parcel from her. 'Didn't I tell you to bring the money? Don't you trust me to buy the stuff myself? What am I? A baby?' He was shouting by now, and Rabbi Zweck tried to calm him. Most of all he wanted to get out of that corridor and be with his son in private. He took Norman's arm. 'Can we go somewhere, a room, perhaps, private, to talk, away from these people?' He could not hide the note of contempt in his voice.

Norman shook his arm free. 'These people,' he echoed, 'these people are my friends and anything I've got to say, they can hear.'

'Hear, hear,' said Minister. 'Don't trust him, do you? Like I said. Families. That's what we got in common. Listen,' he pushed Norman aside. ' 'E's 'im, like I'm me, and all these other blokes are them. My Mum used to bring *me* parcels,' he told Rabbi Zweck confidentially. 'She knew we 'ad the shops, but no, she's got to go and buy it for me. Like I was a baby. Then my Dad died, and I won't let 'er come no more. Poor Dad,' he said almost to himself, 'but at least it was *'is* death. That's more'n you can say for mine. When *I* die, it won't be *my* death, any more'n it's been *my* life. It'll be something that 'appened to my Mum. Shove 'em off,' he said to Norman, 'tell them where they can stick their rotten parcel.'

In face of Minister's attack on his own kin, Norman immediately sided with them, in the same way as he had defended Minister when his father had butted him. 'Let's go in the ward,' he said. He too, wanted a little privacy. If for no other reason than to face one enemy without having to shift his ground.

They followed him into the ward. Bella still held the parcel. Rabbi Zweck trailed behind. What Minister had said had wounded him deeply, too profoundly for him even to begin to analyse why. One thing was certain, cure or no cure, he had to get Norman out of this place. He had to find Norman's source. That was imperative, then he had to get Norman home and look after him there. Suddenly he wanted to go home right away, and back to Norman's bedroom, and start the search in earnest. But he knew that once confronted with those drawers, he would recoil.

Bella had already reached Norman's bed, and he watched his son as he climbed between the sheets. Bella put the parcel on the bed table, and drew up a chair for her father. So they sat on either side of the bed, not daring to look at each other. A few patients paced the ward, up and down between the beds, at a regular largo pace, like sad metronomes. One of them, the chess player, a board under his arm, made as if to come towards Norman's bed.

'Go away,' Norman shouted. The man swerved automatically to the centre and resumed his regular beat. Norman did not want any interference. It was true that they sat there, the three of them, without any communication, but even that was private, their non-words and non-looks, inviolate.

Rabbi Zweck shifted in his chair. He looked up and willed his son to look at him. 'Hullo, Norman,' he said. He had rehearsed it all the way from the bus-stop and it had to come out. It was as if he was prepared to discount their unfortunate initial encounter, and this moment, as far as he was concerned, marked the beginning of his visit.

'Hullo, Pop. How are you?'

'He asks *me*,' Rabbi Zweck smiled. 'You're in the bed, you're in the hospital, and you ask me, how am I. Bella bought you a little parcel, Norman,' he said gently. 'Open it a little. Bella wrapped it so nice. Here,' he stretched over and picked up the package. 'Open it, I should also like to see inside it. A surprise, perhaps.'

'Pop, I'm not a baby, and I'm not moved by surprises. I know what's inside. It's chocolate, I suppose, and shaving stuff. But I could have bought it all myself, here, in our shop.'

Rabbi Zweck shuddered at his son's possessiveness.

'I asked you for the money,' Norman was saying.

'Open it, open it.' Rabbi Zweck insisted, as he himself began to untie the wrapping. The chocolates were first visible, and Rabbi Zweck pulled out the decorated box. 'Such chocolates you got in *your* shop?' He threw his son's sense of property back at him with contempt. He pulled out a packet of sweets. 'Such sweets you can buy? Such shaving lotion? My, my, such soap? Now tell me,' he leaned over the bed, 'such good things you can buy in your shop?'

Norman watched the articles as they fell one by one on his bed. He reckoned the value of each of them, and totted up their total. By his reckoning, it would have accounted for four days white supply. He felt sick at the waste of it all. 'Chocolate,' he almost vomited, 'whoever can eat so much chocolate. And since when did I use this cissy stuff on my face?'

'You asked for chocolate,' Bella said firmly. 'You begged for chocolate. On the phone this morning you pleaded for it like a baby.'

'Like a baby,' Norman repeated. 'That's how you want me, isn't it?' he said bitterly. He fingered the items on the bed, and considered with growing panic what further excuse he could use to get money out of them. Bella's handbag was lying at the foot of the bed. He did not dismiss its possibilities. But he had qualms about it. He had stolen before, often, and usually from the till in the shop. But that was different. You opened the till at least three dozen times during the day. Taking from it could almost be accidental. But a handbag was something different. It involved planning, finger dexterity, in which Norman had had little practice. Nevertheless, it was a possibility, and perhaps the only one open to him.

As if reading his thoughts, Bella stretched over and picked up her bag and opened it. Norman leaned over in an attempt to see inside. There was hardly any point in taking a risk if there were nothing in the bag worth taking. As she pulled out a handkerchief, Norman saw a large open bank envelope. It was the half day's takings in the shop, and because they had come to visit him, Bella had had no time to go to deposit the money. He reckoned on past experience, that a half a day's takings in the shop, especially on early closing day, would amount to something like fifteen pounds. A fortnight's supply. He had to have the money, and they deserved to lose it, bringing his chocolates and shaving lotion as if he were an invalid. He worked up a sizeable hatred for them, to make the theft easier. But there was still the practical problem of getting it into his hands. Bella might want to go to the lavatory, he thought, but then, it was natural that she should take her bag with her. So if it were to be done at all, it had to be done right there, under her nose, and just before they decided to leave, which would give her no time to miss it. He watched her put her handkerchief back, not disturbing the envelope which it covered, and once again, placed the bag at the foot of the bed.

'Thanks for the chocolate, Bella,' he said. 'I'm sorry I was angry. You're good to me, Bella.'

Rabbi Zweck smiled at this display of sibling affection, that occasional bonus of parenthood, and innocent of Norman's reasoning that it was safer, if less ethical, to rob a friend rather than an enemy.

'How's the shop?' he went on. 'Managing without me?'

'You were such a help,' Bella joked.

For a while, they bantered together, with the occasional contribution from Rabbi Zweck. Small talk, positively small, to postpone the real matter of their visit, or perhaps to avoid it altogether. As they talked, Norman wiggled his toes, then his feet, and afterwards, his calves, allowing a decent interval to elapse between each movement, and claiming itchiness from the institution pyjamas that he wore, while all the while, Bella's bag inched its way spasmodically up his legs, till it was within grasping distance of his hands. At each completed stage of the journey, he dwelt at length on what he had learned of the hospital and the stories of the few patients he already knew, and when the bag arrived, he joyously recounted his feeling of well-being.

Bella had all the while watched the bag move, hypnotized by its slow unsteady passage. She made no effort to retrieve it, half knowing where and why it was going. As it balanced on Norman's knee, she totted up the morning's takings and wondered how she could replace them without letting her father know. She was fascinated to discover how Norman would finally achieve his purpose, and she half turned her chair away from him to make the theft easier. She smiled to herself. Norman was showing signs of the old normality which over the years she had learned to accommodate. He'll start sniffing in a moment or two, she thought, and he'll ask me for a handkerchief, and hardly was the thought out, than Norman prepared for his role with a fit of coughing. The sniffing followed as the a cough subsided and Rabbi Zweck muttered. 'Also a cold you have.'

'Also to what?' Norman's firm conviction of his own state of sanity never left him.

'Nothing, nothing,' Rabbi Zweck said quickly.

'Also to what?' Norman insisted.

'I also have a cold,' Rabbi Zweck alibied. 'Also to me,' he explained feebly.

Norman let it pass. With the thought of a fortnight's supply within his reach, he could afford to step down. He sniffed again. 'Have you got a handkerchief, Bella?'

'Here,' Rabbi Zweck said. 'Have mine.' He drew his white handkerchief from his inside pocket.

'You have a cold, Poppa,' Bella said quickly. And she winked at him, in token of her understanding. Rabbi Zweck was grateful for what he took to be her participation in his deception, and he stuffed his handkerchief away. 'There's one in my bag,' Bella said.

Norman opened it, and as he did so, Bella crossed to the other side of the bed, and with her back to Norman, masking her father, she neatly folded his handkerchief and replaced it in his pocket. She looked round to check that Norman's task was accomplished. One hand was under his pillow, while with the other, he blew his nose. It was all clear and she returned to her chair. She left the bag where it was, and did not intend to remove it until they were ready to leave. She would give her brother that much peace.

The garden visitors were now dribbling into the ward. Restless with the open spaces, no doubt infected by their members' needs for confinement, they had happily acquiesced and escorted them to the security of their beds. One patient belonged in the bed next to Norman, and his family followed him there, watched him into bed and tucked him in with exaggerated solicitude. Then they sat around him, making sure that he was not looking at them, so that they could cast surreptitious glances at the ward clock and wonder that the time could pass so slowly. They checked with their watches, as if asylum time had its own discipline, its hours regulated by its watchers' fantasies, spinning weeks in a minute, or grinding out a year with one single shudder of the second hand. They wished there were a limit on visiting hours, like in any sane hospital. But here, departure was left to the relatives' discretion, whatever that word had come to mean in such a place.

There was silence between them, a silence that spread over the adjoining bed where Rabbi Zweck sat with Bella, avoiding Norman's eye. The mother of the boy caught Rabbi Zweck as he glanced at her. 'It's a lovely day today,' she said.

'Yes, Rabbi Zweck said politely, 'is a lovely day.' He too, was glad of the diversion.

100

'I've not seen you here before,' she said. 'Is this your first time?'

'Yes,' Bella joined the conversation. 'I've not been here before.'

'Oh, it's *nice* here,' the woman said. 'I look forward to coming. It's quite an outing for us. I've made quite a few friends here over the years. Met some lovely people. I shall miss it all when he comes out.' Rabbi Zweck shuddered.

'They come and they go,' the woman went on, 'but we seem to go on for ever.' She giggled, half embarrassed. Rabbi Zweck shifted his chair to avoid her bonhomie.

'How long . . .?' Rabbi Zweck started.

'What is it now, George?' she said, 'it'll be six or seven years come September. No, it's six, George,' she rambled on, without George's contradiction. 'I know it's six,' she turned to Rabbi Zweck, 'because it's six years ago that I started running my stall for the children's bazaar. You know, every Christmas we have a bazaar in aid of the orphanage,' she confided. 'I started the stall, because Billy gave me the idea. Didn't you, Billy love?' she turned to the sad heap between the sheets, a man full of thirty years, and surely by now entitled to William. Billy nodded obediently. He even managed a smile, although its target was not his mother. 'The first thing he made – and he'd only been here a few weeks,' the mother went on, 'was a lovely waste-paper basket. It was beautiful, and Billy gave it me for the bazaar. And every week when I came, he'd made something else, so I've collected them for a stall of my own every Christmas. Billy's Bazaar, I call it,' she said, 'and I sell out every time. George, reach me my bag.'

George passed over a large hold-all, and his wife, with great care drew out a plastic lampshade. 'Now, isn't that pretty,' she said, 'I could sell it a hundred times over. Look how he's finished it off,' she thumbed the edges for Bella's perusal, thinking more appreciation would come from that quarter. 'Like a woman's work,' she said proudly. 'Of course, they get all facilities here,' she chatted on, 'and the best instructors. Nothing but the best in materials and so on.'

Bella turned her back slightly. She was thoroughly bored by

the woman, and faintly irritated by an uncomfortable feeling that both she and her father were being used. Rabbi Zweck had long ceased to listen to the woman's chatter. The information that Billy had been there for six years had switched him off entirely. For a moment he had panicked that Norman had Billy's complaint, but he tried to shrug it off. Not to wonder the poor boy was *meshugga,* he thought, with a mother like that. Yet it nagged him to know what was wrong with the boy, what possible malady had kept him there for six long years. He didn't want to know exactly what it was; he had no morbid curiosity about the boy's condition. He just wanted to make sure it wasn't for drugs. 'So long is not for the pills,' he prayed silently. He had to get the woman on one side and ask her. But that would be an act of intimacy, and although he knew she would willingly respond to it, he didn't want to belittle himself by asking her. He would approach the father, man to man. It was better that way. Leave Bella to talk to the woman. He got up and moved towards Billy's bed. He would get to George through Billy, the waste-paper basket maker, whose life was measured out in his wretched mother's bazaars.

'You feel better today?' he said. He wanted to call him by his name, but 'Billy' made him feel foolish.

Billy seemed astonished by the question. 'This is your first visit?' he asked.

Rabbi Zweck nodded. He felt like a new boy who didn't know the ropes.

'After six years,' Billy said, 'people forget you were ever ill. They don't ask you any more if you're getting better. After such a long time, this place isn't a hospital. It's your home.'

Rabbi Zweck was torn by the man's tone of resignation. He wanted to say something kind to him, to bolster him a little, to give him a little dignity, to un-Billy him. He wanted to praise his lampshade, but instinctively he knew that Billy was indifferent to his handiwork, and probably there was nothing in the whole universe that could make Billy care.

'Don't you *want* to go home?' Rabbi Zweck said helplessly.

'This is my home,' Billy said. 'It's used to me here. It provides for me, and towards it, I have no obligation.'

Rabbi Zweck looked at George, and felt something of his own heartache in the father's helpless stare. 'But why should he stay in this place?' Rabbi Zweck said angrily. He was not really putting the question he had meant to ask, he was just protesting against the cardinal sin of the father's blind acceptance. 'Why he should stay? Why? What's the matter with him?' he panicked. He was worried that Norman would catch Billy's submission. Surrender was contagious. He wanted Billy's discharge as much as he wanted his own son's. 'What's the matter with him then, he should stay so long?' There was a pause. Billy looked at his father and stretching out his hand, he touched his father's arm, and drew him towards the bed. Billy could endure his own unhappiness, but not the burden of his father's misery. 'Any day now, they'll find a cure for it, won't they, Dad. They're experimenting all the time. I'm an old guinea-pig, aren't I, Dad.' He punched at his coat sleeve, and laughed. 'You wait,' he said, suddenly cheerful, 'come next Christmas, and Mum'll have to find someone else to provide for her stall.'

'That's right son,' George said, 'come Christmas, and your mother'll go a-begging.' He joined in with Billy's laughter, playfully punching him back.

'Now, now, you lads,' Billy's mother turned back to the bed, 'stop it, George, or you'll make him too excited.'

George stopped it. Both he and his wife knew the outcome of excitement. Excitement was a euphemism they shared for one of Billy's 'turns', and even Rabbi Zweck heard in the word a faint ring of threat and fear. Rabbi Zweck and Billy's mother made to changes places, and in their crossing, the woman pulled Rabbi Zweck aside. 'Don't worry,' she said to him, 'they'll get him off the pills here. In no time. I wish it was as simple with my Billy.'

Rabbi Zweck sat down in the chair by Norman's bed. He'd had his answer. Although he didn't know the nature of Billy's illness, he knew that it was not the same as Norman's and he thanked God for it.

'Bella,' Billy's mother called over. Rabbi Zweck was displeased with the woman's familiarity. 'Come over,' she called, 'George, show the young lady the wallet Billy made for you.'

Bella was obliged to go over and Rabbi Zweck found himself alone with Norman.

'You finished with that lot?' Norman said. While his father had been over at Billy's bed, and Bella had been devoured by Billy's mother, he had felt like a host, ignored, and a terrible sense of isolation had overcome him. Again he had the sudden urge to get out of the place, despite the security of a fortnight's supply. They were all mad in here, and he would become like them. He wanted to go home. They had to get him out of there. Rabbi Zweck saw tears in Norman's eyes. He leaned over and whispered. 'A nice boy, that – er – Billy. A very nice boy.'

'Pop,' Norman said, 'I want to go home. Please take me home.' His tears were running freely now, and Rabbi Zweck looked frantically to Bella for support. 'I'll try,' he said feebly, 'but you give it a chance. A few weeks,' he dared.

'I can't, I can't,' Norman said. 'Let me come home. And Auntie Sadie'll look after me. I'll come off the drugs. I promise you.' He held his father by the shoulders. 'I promise,' he said, 'you must take me home.'

'I'll see, I'll see,' Rabbi Zweck said.

'Yes, but see now. Go and see the doctor now.'

'Bella, Bella,' Rabbi Zweck called, angry that she was not to support him. 'Bella, come over. He wants to go home,' he said helplessly, as she reached the bed.

'Please, please, Bella,' Norman cried, 'take me home. Please. Tell them to let me go.'

Bella looked at her father. Each depended on the other to remain firm. Rabbi Zweck would forgive Bella for keeping him in this place, and likewise Bella would forgive her father. But both of them wanted him home, but both knew that he was committed, a month at least, that's what the gentleman with the briefcase had said. Yet neither dared tell Norman.

'Try a few weeks, a month,' Rabbi Zweck spelled it out. 'After a month you come home, you hear,' he raised his voice, 'better or no better,' he said to the ward in general. 'You come home. Enough of this,' he said. 'A month, then home. I promise.'

'Why a month?' Norman cried.

Bella was afraid that he had guessed at his sentence. A month was a word with an undeniable legal ring. 'Three, four weeks,' she said casually. 'We'll see how it goes. I promise you, me and Poppa, we'll take you home.'

'Please, please,' Norman begged.

Rabbi Zweck looked at the ward clock. Whatever the time, he had to get away. He had to get back to Norman's bedroom. There was no time to be lost. Of one thing he was certain. Norman had to get out of this place. But in order to care for him at home, he had to find his source, he had to cut it off once and for all. 'We must go,' he said suddenly.

'Why?' Norman demanded.

Rabbi Zweck could think of no reason, acceptable or otherwise. 'We must go,' he repeated.

'You're running away, aren't you?' Norman said.

'Of course not,' Bella said quickly. 'It's a strain on Poppa. You know it is, Norman. We'll come again. Soon,' she added.

'Don't put yourself to any inconvenience,' he said. He slid down between the sheets, displaying his distress, so that they could hold the image of his agony as they left the ward. He wasn't going to make it easy for them. But Rabbi Zweck didn't look at him. He knew that what he would see, he could not bear. He started to walk away.

'Good-bye, Pop,' he heard. Norman's voice froze him where he stood, and he turned and went back to the bed. 'Don't worry,' he said, kissing him. 'I'll arrange, I'll arrange. You'll be home. Auntie Sadie will come. You'll be better.' He turned away quickly, and made his blurred way out of the ward.

Outside in the tea corridor, he waited. He hoped that Bella would stay and comfort Norman for a while. He sat at one of the tables opposite the little room where only yesterday, Norman had been admitted. Now the door opened, and the nurse, who had then comforted him, came out and approached the table. 'He's a little better, today,' he said.

Rabbi Zweck smiled feebly.

'You mustn't let it get you down,' the nurse went on. 'Next time you come, bring him some outdoor clothes. He might feel better, dressed. Peck him up a bit.'

'No,' Rabbi Zweck said. He hadn't meant to sound so decisive. But a suit of clothes in this place was out of the question.

He was not going to have his son settling in, moving in bag and baggage to a place like this. 'No,' he said less firmly. 'The day he comes out, I'll bring the clothes.'

The nurse went back to his room, and came out again, carrying Norman's dressing-gown. 'You can take this home,' he said gently. 'We provide them here.'

Rabbi Zweck took the garment without a word. The nurse patted his arm and went off down the corridor. Rabbi Zweck held the gown at arm's length. It looked bequeathed, the sleeves still rolled up, as if lately inhabited. Rabbi Zweck folded it quickly on his lap. Idly he felt in the pocket. A crumpled handkerchief and a scrap of paper. He pulled the paper out. It was folded into a neat square. He tried to fight off that same surge of nausea that he had felt while rummaging the drawers. The empty gown looked innocent enough, yet here he was, going through the pockets, as if his son were dead. But it might contain a clue. 'Who knows?' he muttered to himself. He spread the paper on the table and unfolded it. 'Basement Flat', it read, and underneath there was an address and a telephone number. Across the bottom of the paper was written in his son's handwriting, 'Not Fridays.'

Rabbi Zweck folded the paper quickly and put it in his inside pocket. He patted his waistcoat with supreme confidence. 'The murderer,' he muttered to himself. He was overjoyed with his find, but he had to keep it from Bella. He himself would follow the clue. He would find the man at the end of that telephone number, he would . . . 'No no,' he said to himself. 'Let me just find him, that's all. I should only find him and stop him. Just stop him.' He patted his find again. 'Murderer,' he whispered, but he smiled gently, for having found him, he had already half forgiven him.

Now he was impatient for Bella to join him. He had to get home and start his inquiries. Occasionally, a visitor would leave the ward, slowly at first, and then with relief, with quickened pace, out of the building. Billy's parents came out into the corridor and did not look back to the ward. His mother held the plastic lampshade above her head, like a trophy. They nodded to Rabbi Zweck as they passed. 'See you next visit,' George said. The man shrugged his shoulders helplessly. He wanted it no more than Rabbi Zweck, yet he knew that a further meeting between them was inevitable.

Bella came out shortly afterwards. 'Don't worry,' she said, almost before she reached him. 'I've told him we're going to get him out. He's calm now. Poppa,' she said going closer to him. 'This is no place for him. We must get him home. He'll go mad in there.'

'Yes, yes,' Rabbi Zweck said. 'We will, we will. First we find where he gets them. Then we bring him home.'

'But we'll never find out,' Bella said.

'We will, we will.' He was sorely tempted to divulge his latest clue, but he felt a certain excitement about it, which at the moment he didn't want to share. 'We will, we will,' he said again, and Bella wondered at her father's conviction.

They walked to the bus-stop in silence. Rabbi Zweck told himself that he would go out that evening to the address on the paper, but where, he wondered, would he tell Bella he was going. He would have, God forgive him, to make up some story. Bella, on the other hand, was indulging in her own secret, and wondering how she could replace the shop money before her father noticed it was missing.

Billy's parents were already waiting at the stop. As he approached them, Rabbi Zweck saw that Billy's mother, her face buried in a large handkerchief, was weeping uncontrollably. At her side, George stood bewildered, holding the lampshade till she cried herself out. Then when the bus arrived, he gently guided her inside. Rabbi Zweck followed them. He recollected the woman's tiresome behaviour in the ward, but now he saw it as a token of strength. He put his hand on the back of George's coat as they walked to their seats. George turned and nodded an acknowledgement. 'It's the strain,' he said. 'It's the constant worry of it all.'

'I know, I know,' Rabbi Zweck said. In *tzorras* he needed no lessons.

11

Rabbi Zweck got off the bus at the beginning of the park. It was already dark, and the nature of his adventure and his un-familiar surroundings, both frightened and excited him. He turned up the collar of his coat, and looked furtively about him. A passer-by might have thought that the Rabbi was acting out his own private fantasy of private detective. He padded along the pavement, keeping close to the wall. Occasionally he re-peated the address to himself. A hundred and three was a good walk ahead, a hundred and three houses to be precise, since the road was a one-sided dwelling one. He hoped that the man would be at home and that his business was not restricted to the day-time. He could have phoned of course. But when he'd thought about it, he didn't want to warn the man of his coming. He would catch him red-handed, unawares.

He had not prepared his reason for going out, and when Bella asked him, as he was buttoning his coat, he was astonished at how easily the lie had come. 'Mrs Golden invited me. This morning in the shop. I should go for supper. But I said, after supper I should come. Why should I eat with Mrs Golden when in the house we have plenty.' He was over-elaborating, and he was aware of his miserable performance. It was a story that was easily checkable. He hoped Bella wouldn't believe it, but would trust that his journey, wherever it was, was necessary. She had smiled at him and helped him on with his coat. She knew that his journey had something to do with Norman, but she was angry that Norman had reduced her father to lying on his behalf. Where would it all end? When Rabbi Zweck had gone, she had stood watching him over the well of the staircase. She shuddered at the thought of how involved they had both become in her brother's madness. How they had become know-ing receivers, as it were, from a thief. That she had allowed, even encouraged Norman to take the shop money, knowing full well why he wanted it. That her father, perhaps even now, was negotiating to get Norman out of that place, when they both knew that it was for his own good that he should stay there. They could not bear to make him miserable, though if she were honest, it was her own pain and her father's that was unsupportable. And so they had both entered Norman's derangement, making it workable, tidying it even, making it all 'nice'. They were both equally guilty. She knew in her heart, it was better for strangers to look after him. Her answer over the years to Norman's sickness had been that he was doing it on purpose to drive them all crazy. She had to be angry with him. It was the surest hold on her own sanity. If a mind wavered, it was best to keep the kin at bay.

Rabbi Zweck stopped to check the number of the house he had reached. Twenty-five. He still had a long way to go. He reckoned that he had already walked at least twice the length of his own home block, and that encompassed at least thirty houses. But none of the terraced houses in his neighbourhood had the luxuries of spacious front gardens and side-entrances. Where he lived, neighbourliness was not necessarily an act of friendship; it was something that was geographically inevitable. Here, he wondered whether it existed at all.

When he'd left the flat, his mood had been angry, and he was determined to punish his son's supplier. But now, as he neared the house, his eagerness for battle diminished. He was conscious too of his own frailty, and his complete ignorance of the world he was about to enter. And even if he could stop up this source, he reflected, what guarantee was there that Norman wouldn't find another? Perhaps it would be better after all to leave him in the hospital, but the thought of Billy and all the other *meshuggoyim* once again determined Norman's release. 'Ach,' he mumbled, 'any way is bad, Out, in. Is both terrible.'

At last, he arrived, panting a little, at number one hundred and three, and he stopped outside, gripping the gate to steady his trembling body. 'Forgive me, forgive,' he muttered as he made his way down the steps to the basement.

There was a light behind the door. There was someone at

home, and Rabbi Zweck hesitated before ringing the bell. He looked up the main steps and could barely see the main street. He felt trapped and frightened. Almost without realizing it, he pressed the bell as if to beg admission to his fear and the opportunity to deal with it.

The door opened as an automatic response to the bell. He hesitated. Admission was too easy. He would have wanted to be denied, so at least he could have protested from the very beginning. As he hesitated the door closed.

He paused to think before ringing the bell again. But what was there to think about. He had to do it, and get it over with, and the less thought, the better. Any kind of consideration would have been an impediment. What he was doing was irrational and unlikely to lead to anything fruitful. But he had to do it. He had to make just one positive gesture, even if only for his own sake. All he had donated to the situation, was his own heartache, an ingrowing pain that fed on its own turnings.

He pressed the bell defiantly and put his foot ready for the opening door. He was inside before the door had swung its full width, and he walked forward along a narrow corridor. The corridor itself was in darkness, but at its end Rabbi Zweck could see a blaze of light that spread over a wider area. A flight of carpet stairs sprouted from the centre of the room, and faded into blackness as if it led nowhere. He looked about him. There were two small tables spread with magazines, and large ceramic ashtrays. Scattered around were hard-backed chairs. Since he was waiting for the doctor, he decided that he would sit down, and he hoped that eventually someone would come and see to him. He grew impatient, afraid that he might weaken and slip out the way he had come. He gripped the arms of the chair, holding himself down, trying to rehearse the beginning of what he would say. 'Doctor, is about my son,' he tried. Yes, that would do; he would settle on that. It was a polite introduction, an apology for whatever abuse should come into his mind. He refrained from rehearsing further. 'Doctor, is about my son,' he repeated to himself.

He heard footsteps that seemed to come from the black height of the stairs. Now it was his turn, and he made to get up from his chair. A man's legs came through the darkness, and as they descended, Rabbi Zweck saw a slightly built figure, rather younger than he had envisaged for a doctor, fair-haired, dishevelled, and obviously in a great hurry. His haste spurred Rabbi Zweck to his feet, and without meaning to, he blocked the man's path to the other corridor... 'Doctor, is about...' Rabbi Zweck began.

'I can't help you. I don't live here,' the man said hurriedly. He was dodging Rabbi Zweck's timid barrier. He was obviously anxious to get away. He slipped past him. '*I* don't live here,' he shouted back from the corridor, as if this were the main piece of information he wanted to put across. Rabbi Zweck heard the flat-door slam, and the man running up the steps to the street.

He sat down again and waited, glad of the respite, and already weary from the false start. He was tired. The long walk from the bus-stop was beginning to throb in his legs. He closed his eyes, shutting out the distaste and fear of what he was doing, and gave himself fully to the fatigue that slowly overcame him. He knew he was going to sleep, but he didn't care.

Almost as soon as he shut his eyes, he saw Norman smiling at him. He knew he was dreaming, but he held on to his sleep, and the heartening image that it had delivered. 'Pop,' Norman said, 'look what I've got for you.' He was sitting up in his bed, smiling, his hands underneath the blankets, hiding something. 'Turn around,' he said, 'and don't look till I tell you,' he said. 'It's a surprise.' Rabbi Zweck turned from the bed and looked around the ward. It was empty except for one bed at the far end of the room by the door. Propped up on the pillow was a lamp-shade reading a book, and the light flickered on and off as it turned the pages. 'Now.' Norman shouted behind him. Rabbi Zweck turned round. Propped on the bed was a waste-paper basket. Norman clasped it proudly. 'I made it,' he said. 'I made it for you, Pop.' Rabbi Zweck took the waste-paper basket from him. 'I can't lift it,' he said. 'Is very heavy.' Norman laughed and snuggled down between the sheets. As he did so, the basket rolled off on to the floor. 'Of course you can't lift it,' Norman said. 'It's full.' Rabbi Zweck looked at the basket on the floor. It was indeed full. It was full of Billy.

Rabbi Zweck woke up. Not with a start, but slowly, and without any firm conviction that it had only been a dream. He quickly orientated himself to his whereabouts, and he was angry that he had not been attended to. He got up and made his way to the foot of the stairs. 'Hullo, hullo,' he shouted. He was astonished at the panic in his voice. He knew that his short sleep had frightened him, but he couldn't remember why. He was only conscious of a hang-over of intense anger. He mounted two steps. 'Hullo,' he shouted again. He heard a rustling at the top of the stairs and he retreated quickly back to his chair. He tried to remember what he had rehearsed for the doctor, but it had gone completely.

He regretted his angry outburst. It was a bad beginning. He tried to appear casual, turning his back on the stairway. He heard more movements from the upper floor, and idly he picked up a magazine and flicked over the pages. He saw picture after picture of naked girls, and he felt he was still dreaming. Such pictures could never inhabit a doctor's waiting-room. He had to pull himself together. He threw the magazine down in disgust. He was prepared to acknowledge that it hadn't been there, that he hadn't seen it, that he'd never come to this place, and that he'd better go and erase the whole happening from his mind. He walked towards the outer corridor.

'Yes?' a voice said behind him.

He looked around. At the foot of the stairs, draped over the banister, in an attitude of utter fatigue, was a woman. To Rabbi Zweck, she seemed to have emerged hurriedly. He stared at her. He waited for her to speak again, for he was still not confident of his own full consciousness, and he was not sure that he had completely shaken off his terrifying sleep. 'Yes?' she said again.

'Is about my son,' he said.

'Come up,' she said. She turned languidly and slouched wearily up the stairs. As she neared the top, she turned around, and saw him still standing there. 'Come on then,' she said. 'We haven't got all night.'

He moved, bewildered. He assumed that the woman was the doctor's wife, or perhaps his assistant and that the doctor's surgery was on the next floor. But he was disturbed by the woman's appearance. It was unclean. And those magazines. They too, had nothing to do with medicine. But he followed her, hanging on to the banister and quickening his pace as she threatened to disappear into the darkness. At the top of the stairs, he had to grope his way behind her. Then a beam of light flushed the darkness. She had opened a door and she stood aside for him to pass through. He moved into the light and hesitated on the threshold. Facing him was an unmade bed, a broken lampshade, and a heap of clothes on a chair. 'After you,' she said, with exaggerated politeness.

Rabbi Zweck had now given up all hope of seeing a doctor, but he still managed to shut out the truth of the situation from his mind. He went inside. The room was smaller than he had expected. In fact, most of its space was taken up by the bed he had already seen. Otherwise, there was a small chest of drawers, another chair, and in the corner, a dirty sink. He fastened his eyes on the bowl of the sink, hoping to get a grip on himself. He saw a long black single hair, and he followed its length to the sink hole. He wanted very much to be sick. The woman closed the door behind her.

'Doctor,' he said, and it sounded ridiculous, 'is about my son.'

'What's this doctor, son business?' she said. She seemed to have woken up a little. She took a dirty hair brush from off the bed and tugged it through her hair.

'You are not a doctor,' Rabbi Zweck stated rather than questioned. He wanted to convince her that it had all been a mistake.

'Do I look like a doctor?' she said smiling. She could see his distress. 'What is it?' she said, going across to him. He did not back away, as he would have expected of himself. Instead, he was overwhelmingly grateful for her concern. He wanted to sit down and cry it all out, the weary story of why he had come, of Norman in hospital, of Billy in the next bed, of Billy's mother, weeping at the bus-stop, but most of all, he wanted to cry out his own shame. He moved towards the unladen chair, and made to sit down. She grabbed him by the shoulders, laughing. 'It's broken,' she said, 'that one. Come and sit on the bed.'

He let himself be led across to the bed, and he sank down wearily, feeling no repulsion at the dirty sheets and the pile of worn clothing strewn over the bundled blankets. She stood over him and made no move to sit down. He noticed for the first time, that she was wearing a dressing-gown, and he smiled to himself as he watched her pick up the ends of the belt, and make a double knot. He saw it was a gesture of respect, and he was grateful for it.

'What is it?' she said, 'this son of yours? What's the matter with him?'

He didn't hear her question. He was looking at the cleavage between the lapels of her dressing-gown. In spite of the double knot she had tied at her waist, the gown fell open around the breasts. Rabbi Zweck stared at them. She was not young. She reminded him reluctantly of Sarah, because he knew of no other comparison. The wrinkled skin on her neck puckered down her chest and small clusters of black spots occasionally flattened the creases. He could smell her, with a distinct mixture of smells that he had known long ago, and which now came back to him with exciting nostalgia. First, his poor Sarah, God rest her soul, as she came out of a bath, and then with distinct association, the smell of the stables where he and his elder brothers had, years ago, washed down his father's horses. The servant smell from the attic rooms, in preparation for the evening out, she embodied them all, this woman who now bent over him, and nostalgia blunted the edge of his disgust. 'My son,' he started again.

'Yes, and what about your son?' There was a slight hint of impatience in her voice. 'Let's get him over with.' She bent down farther, so that one breast fell out of her dressing-gown. Rabbi Zweck watched it emerge without surprise. He looked at it closely. It looked as if it needed ironing. He thought of the pictures in the magazine downstairs, but this flesh had nothing to do with those glossy swellings. Those had disgusted him. But this was different. Perhaps once her breast had been full and round, but now it was a deflated appendage, and its exposure had been accidental. He raised his hand and noticed that he still had his gloves on. Slowly he pulled one off, finger by finger, and then he cupped the loose breast in his hand, and he put it away. Then he replaced his glove and folded his hands in his lap.

'You're quite a dirty old man, aren't you,' she said, straightening herself.

'I . . .' he began, but he realized there was no point in an explanation. For a moment, while sitting on the bed, he had felt more relaxed than he could remember for a long time, and she had broken it for him. Now he could not help but look upon her for what she was, and he felt sickened that Norman had had dealings with her. 'Why did he come to you, my son?' he asked.

'I'm the Citizens' Advice Bureau,' she said disdainfully. 'What d'you think he came to see me for? Why have you come, anyway. That would be more to the point.'

Rabbi Zweck got up from the bed. He wanted to get away. It had been a fruitless journey and a shameful one. But the woman seemed in no hurry for him to go. She went across to the rickety chair and sat down on it carefully, leaning backwards and spreading her legs wide to adjust her balance. The dressing-gown fell open both below and above the double knot of her belt. Her legs were shaved to the knees, but above, to the top of her thighs, the mottled skin was covered with straggly hair. The manner in which she sat was not a gesture of invitation; it was clearly the only way the broken chair could be accommodated. But Rabbi Zweck could no longer look upon it as a matter of convenience. As far as the breast was concerned, he had only put it back for tidiness sake, and he had taken his glove off because you didn't touch things with your gloves on. But he didn't want to tidy her up as she sat there. He liked it, the way she was, and he was sick with shame that she so excited him. Not for many, many years, and perhaps, he thought to himself, never in his life, had such hungry tremblings entered his body. He made no attempt to control them, and they were intensified by his own shame. He looked around the room, and found pleasure in the dirty sheets, in the pile of worn clothing on the bed, and in the disgusting filth of the woman's body.

'What was your son's name?' the woman said.

'Was? Was?' Rabbi Zweck asked. 'He *is*, he *is*, my son.'

'What is his name then?'

'Henry,' Rabbi Zweck said quickly. He was astonished at how quickly the name had come to him. It was the name of one of the young assistants he'd had in the shop, whom he'd had to sack because he was always touching Bella.

'I don't know a Henry,' the woman said. 'In any case, they never tell me their real names.'

Rabbi Zweck wondered what name Norman had used, and what name he himself would use if she were to ask him. He found himself moving towards her, and as he neared her, he realized for the first time, that, in spite of a life-time of rigid self-discipline, he had never known temptation. Over the years, he had denied himself, for the sake of family and for the sake of principle, but it had never meant any particular hardship for him. Now for the first time, he knew temptation, and it was his body that threatened to betray him. 'Oh God,' he muttered to himself, hesitating in his steps. 'I'm an old man. For so long I live without, for so long I never even wanted. Why now should I want?' He felt himself sweating. He stood still. He was in no hurry to reach her. Temptation had a sweet joy, that he was savouring for the first time. He wondered how many other joys had been denied him. All the circumstances of his life, his dead wife, Bella, his married daughter, and his lunatic son, all had obligingly faded from his mind; all he was aware of was his steaming body. He moved to her side.

'What's your son look like?' the woman said. 'I probably know which one he is. I only oblige a few customers.'

Her question froze him. For a short while, while his body had held dominion, all else had lost its sway, and now, with her reminder, he saw Norman in the hospital bed, the small square of paper in his dressing-gown, and the woman's room which was here and now that had to be dealt with. He backed away from her, horrified by the thought that he might have shared her with his son, and the lust that had lately licked through his body, now tongued it with shame. His knees watered with his humiliation. He touched the woman's shoulder. She was blameless. From time to time, she had made his Norman happy, and for that he thanked her.

'I'll go,' he said. 'I'm sorry. A mistake. We all make mistakes. Is my fault,' he said, seeing her questioning look. 'Someone else I thought you were. But is not you.' He walked towards the door and turned around. 'You are kind,' he said. 'Very kind. I'm sorry, but is a mistake I made.' He opened the door, and left it ajar, so that the light from the room would guide him down the dark stairs. He went as quickly as he could through the waiting-room and down the corridor to the front door.

Breathlessly, he mounted the basement steps, and once in the clean fresh air outside, he leaned against the railings and tried to cope with the cooling of his body and the heat of his shame. He panted there for a while, then wearily walked away. He walked close to the wall, his shame stabbing him, and he tightened the muscles of his neck, so that a fierce grin spread over his face and with the grimace, he uttered a low animal cry disassociating his shame from his own being. He hurried to the bus-stop. Once on the bus, he would be able to concentrate on the other passengers, on the passing shop windows, on paying his fare, and perhaps even talking to whoever sat next to him.

The bus came mercifully soon. He went inside where there were more people, and he took a seat next to an old man. But at the next stop, the old man got off, and Rabbi Zweck was left sitting alone and staring out of the window. There were no shops on the bus route, and few people in the streets, and the bus emptying with every stop. Walking was better for taking your mind off things, than sitting alone with nothing to see and no one to talk to. 'Ach,' he said aloud, 'what is happening with me. And Norman,' he muttered, 'what is happening.' One or two people turned to look at him, but could find no meaning in his mumblings. They only saw his distress, and turned quickly away. 'Why my son,' he mumbled, 'why my son should go to such a woman? A *nafka*,' he had to say the word. There was only one word for her. It was one of the cards he had to put on the table. And alongside it, he had to put his son. 'My son and a *nafka*,' he muttered. 'Why, why? He couldn't get a nice Yiddische girl?' he asked plaintively. 'Is something wrong with my son he has to pay for it? For pills, for whores he pays. Oi,' he sighed, 'such a life, such a miserable life.'

He leaned back in his seat and shut his eyes. He would soon be home, with his good Bella. He had blessings, after all. Should he not count them. He dozed until he reached his stop. As he left the bus, he felt people looking at him. He didn't care. 'My good Bella,' he kept saying to himself. It was an anchor that would tide him home.

He put his key in the door. Bella was waiting up for him.

117

Rabbi Zweck was not a demonstrative man, but he rushed to her and held her in his arms.

'Are you all right, Poppa?' she said.

'Yes, good, good.'

'How was Mrs Golden?'

'Mrs Golden?' He had entirely forgotten his excuse. 'Oh well, well. Like she always is. Is hot water for a bath?' he said quickly.

'I'll get it ready,' Bella said.

In the bathroom, he noted the clean towel, freshly laundered and laid out for him, the steaming water, his dressing-gown and slippers ready. They were all blessings. One day, please God, Norman would be home again. So what if he goes now and then with a *nafka*?

He took off his clothes. He ignored his body as he stepped into the bath. For many years now, he had been indifferent to his flesh, but tonight he positively avoided looking at it. He wanted to wash it clean. Not from her. No. He thanked her for what she had been able to give his son. It was not her filth and smell that he would rub away. That was hers, and she had earned it in her honest way. He himself had to be clean to earn his blessings.

12

It was the commotion in the ward, the scurry of feet, the cheers and boos of the patients, the overall discord that nudged Norman's sleep. He tossed and groaned a little, then woke, sweating. In his first few days in hospital, he would wake up and wonder where he was and why he was there. He would take his time to realize his whereabouts, because he knew somewhere in his mind that they were distasteful. Then after a week, he awoke in full knowledge of where he was. And it pained him less. He had an unlimited supply of white, and Bella was always good for a touch. He really had nothing to worry about. Not even to get out of the place worried him any more. He recapped the time he had been there. He no longer counted it in days, like in the beginning. It was about a month, and he was indifferent as to whether it was more or less. It was a life that could be led as long as the white was there.

Only one thing recently had nagged at him. He had begun to see them again. In the night when he could not sleep, he'd asked for a sleeping pill to wipe them away. But he knew while he was sleeping that they were still there. At first he thought he must have brought them in with him on his body, and he feared that the nurses would tell him off for his social indiscretion. He'd asked Billy about them, but Billy couldn't see them. But then, what did Billy know? He was madder than all of them. Minister saw them, or at least he said he saw them, along with lots of other things that even Norman, with his heightened perception could not decipher.

Minister could see their droppings and he said they were enormous. Cow-pads, they were, he said, and how could all these insensitive bastards in the ward, stand the smell of them. He'd kicked them away with his foot, and he'd gone raving around the domestics, yelling at them to clean the bloody place up. He'd threatened to report the whole lot of them to the Cabinet, and have them expelled from the Party. That was over a week ago. They'd put him to sleep, and he was still sleeping. That worried Norman too. He lay there, irritated by the commotion around him, yet too concerned with his own problem to sit up and see what it was all about. What worried him was the continuation of his supply. When Minister went into his sleep, he'd left Norman with a week's worth of white. Tomorrow, his supply would be exhausted. He dare not think of how he'd get through the day, or the next, or the next, if Minister didn't wake up. He began to hate him. 'Cow-pads,' he spat contemptuously, 'cow-pads in the middle of a hospital ward. Lunatic. They ought to put him away.'

Norman touched the sweat on his forehead. He wondered whether every night he sweated through, without knowing it. What were they making such a bloody row about. Can't a man get some sleep around here. Like a bunch of madmen they are, Something landed on his head. He sat bolt-upright in his bed, rubbing his bruised temple. 'What the fuck . . .' he shouted. He opened his eyes and saw one of Billy's lampshades lying on his bed. He picked it up to fling it back, but he saw that Billy's bed was empty and the sheets and mattress were smouldering. All the patients were awake, some running around, chucking water on to the fire, or hiding under their beds or just getting in the way and cheering. All except Minister, who slept through it all, who had enough to sleep away with his own ravings.

'Where's Billy?' Norman shouted. 'Where's a nurse? Where's anybody?' Then he saw him at the far end of the ward. His rigid presence had made a clearing, and those with near-by beds, were underneath them, cowering from his rigidity. The night-nurse, Andrews, new on the ward, and from the probational glint in his eye, probably new to the whole business, stood facing him, a few feet away, mouthing his name, for nothing could be heard above the din and clatter of the other patients to whom any break in the monotony of their lives was to be exploited to the full. Norman got out of bed, and walked down the ward. He stood himself next to Andrews, so that he could look Billy in the face. It was not easy to look at him. The rigidity that had fixed his whole body, seemed to have his eyes as its source; these and these alone, were the only part of him that was still. All the rest, his arms, hands, legs, and shoulders, throbbed with controlled staccato vibrations. His jaw ticked over like a well-oiled engine, with the same regularity, so that, had he been able to speak, he would have spoken ticker-tape.

'Billy,' Andrews was saying. 'Be a good boy, Billy, now.'

Norman could hear the fear in his voice, and there was indeed something terrifying about the machine-like figure that dominated the ward. Andrews made to go towards him, calling his name, exhorting him to be a good boy, whatever he meant by that.

'Get another nurse,' Norman said. 'Shall I go and get one. You can't do it on your own.' He himself was not prepared to help. He was a devout coward, and had sufficient imagination to envisage the outcome of a close-in with Billy in his condition. 'Shall I get help?' he said.

'I'll handle it,' Andrews said. He assumed that this kind of crisis was a normal part of his routine, and it would have been a reflection on his efficiency if he could not handle it alone. 'Be a good boy, now, Billy,' he said again. He stepped forward.

Bloody fool, Norman thought, he won't even take off his glasses. Andrews walked straight towards Billy, and stopped, facing him. Norman could not help but admire the man's courage. Andrews was saying something, probably the same inanities that he had started off with. He was telling Billy to be a good boy, but what right had he, or anyone else to suppose that Billy was being a bad boy. And how could he think that Billy was in any state to understand words, since he had assumed the status of a machine. Then Andrews raised his hand. Norman knew instinctively that it was a fatal move, and he wished again that the man had the sense to take off his glasses. He touched Billy ever so gently on the arm, but it was enough to throw out Billy's whole generator. The rest of his body lost its centre, and stuttered out in spasmodic frenzy. The isolated arm raised itself and landed poor Andrews between the eyes like a curse. Norman heard the thud and a trickle of broken glass. Andrews rocked a little. There was a sudden silence in the ward. The men kept their distance but moved closely towards each other. And as the audience gathered, Andrews fell. Nobody looked at him.

They were watching Billy, who still sputtered away. He looked down at the cramped labours of his arms and legs, and turned his head, offended by his rotten engine. Norman looked down at Andrews. 'Serves you right,' he thought. 'That'll teach you to be a hero.' There was blood on his face, and the bridge of his glasses seemed to have caved into his nose, while the frames projected like broken wings. He went into the nurses' room outside the ward, and rang the first bell he could find. Then he saw McPherson, who shared night duty with Andrews, curled up on the couch, fast asleep. Norman shook him awake. 'There's trouble,' he said. 'Andrews is hurt.'

McPherson shook the sleep off him. He grabbed Norman's pyjama sleeve. 'You're not pulling my leg, are you,' he said.

Norman dusted his hand off. 'See for yourself,' he said, and he strolled out of the room.

McPherson followed him. Andrews still lay there, bleeding. Billy had meantime gathered more momentum. His rhythm had returned, and he was running happily like clockwork. The men stood around and watched with growing melancholy. McPherson took in the scene and went straight over to Andrews. He lifted him up and laid him on the nearest bed. 'Back to bed, all of you,' he shouted. The men felt safer with McPherson there, and even those who had been hiding under their beds, ventured out. McPherson was an old hand at the game. He was kind and firm and he didn't want to punish anybody. He glanced at Billy and went quickly to the ward phone. He muffled his words into the receiver, then he replaced it, and did the round of the ward, skirting Billy and ignoring him. 'Into bed, now,' he said to the stragglers. Norman went back to his own bed, and like the other men, sat up and waited.

'The show's over,' McPherson said. 'It's sleep time. Down you get, all of you.' He was patiently taking the whole situation in his stride. The men lay down, their eyes open, fearful for Billy, and their own isolation. Most of them were thinking of home. McPherson stopped at Andrews' bed. He took a folded towel from the nearest locker and soaked it in the ward sink. With it he tidied up Andrews' face, tut-tutting at the man's inexperience. He tried to dislodge the glasses, but he conceded that that was probably a surgeon's job. And now, though cleaned up, Andrews looked much worse than before. There now seemed no reason for his glasses to be so ridiculously embedded in his face. McPherson smiled slightly and went to the door of the ward to wait. The men pretended to be sleeping, but they watched Billy as he stood there, revving away happily.

The posse arrived very quickly, four of them, and one of the doctors. Some of the nurses must have been sent from other wards, because the men had not seen them before. Slowly they sat up in their beds. The doctor went over to Andrews. He made a sign to two of the nurses, who went out and returned with a stretcher. Andrews was carried out silently and the other nurses watched him go. Fallen in the execution of his duties seemed to be the unanimous comment as he was borne away. 'Poor sod,' one of them said, taking a look at Andrews' battered face, 'he won't be back for a while.'

Until now, Billy had been ignored. The other two nurses, with McPherson, started to make an ostensible round of the ward. At the top of the ward, they assembled. Billy's throbbing back was towards them. Then McPherson selected a large key from his bunch and opened the door behind him. Norman had never seen this door opened, but Minister had told him gruesome stories of what lay behind it. It was knee-deep in cowpads, according to Minister. It was where they finished you off, good and proper. McPherson unlocked the door, and opened it slightly. Then he joined the other two nurses. The men watched them, all now sitting up in their beds. McPherson nodded and the three of them tip-toed silently forward. There was no sound in the ward, except for Minister's light and regular snore. The patients watched the silent assault. Then, as they neared Billy, with instinctive loyalty to one of their number, they shouted to a man, 'Look out, Billy. Look out.'

But Billy's own engine had deafened him and he went on ticking regardless. The nurses were now directly behind him, but Billy was unaware of their proximity. Together they raised their arms over him, and folded him in a casual gesture between them. Together they lifted him, his rigid body slightly raised from the floor between them, his feet stiff, and his toes rigidly pointed. He looked straight ahead of him, though it was doubtful that he could see anything. If he was putting up a struggle, it was invisible. The men held him like three vicious clamps, with a strength that was strangely at odds with the look of extreme gentleness on their faces. When they came to the door, McPherson eased his foot around it, and the four of them went sideways through. The door locked itself as it shut, and though the men strained their ears, they could hear no footsteps from the other side. When it was all over, the men avoided each others' glances. While the show had lasted, they had experienced the elation of survivors, but now there was only a sour taste. Most of them envied Minister, who had given it a miss and whom it had left unscathed. They drew themselves down between the sheets, each of them sharing the aftermath of bitterness, and the nagging fear that one day it would be one of them. None of them dared imagine where Billy had gone. They had barely explored or understood the walls of their own prison.

The incident left Norman deeply depressed. Not that he particularly liked Billy. The fact that his father thought that Billy was a nice boy was enough to make him hostile. In fact, every time his father and Bella came on a visit, they spent most of the time with Billy, not so much out of interest in Billy's condition, but as a ready-to-hand excuse to avoid himself. He turned over and gazed at the empty bed alongside him. The mattress had been taken away together with the sheets, and the blankets were folded neatly over the springs. The whole bed looked discharged from service, as it might have looked if Billy had just died, and Norman was frightened at the speed with which all traces of a man could be removed. He wondered what had happened in the very beginning, how it had all started while he was still asleep. Had Billy set fire to his bed, and who had taken him out of it? And at what point in the whole procedure, had Billy become untouchable. Where was he now, Norman dared to wonder. Was he still encased in his own starched inflexibility, his own self-made strait-jacket? He wished him sleep. That was all that was left for any of them.

He turned over on his other side. He knew that getting back to sleep would be impossible. He heard the others tossing along the line of bedding. Someone on the far side was sobbing. Norman cursed him for not having the decency to stifle the helplessness that all of them were trying to contain in their sleepless beds. He turned again, keeping his eyes shut all the time, because he knew they were there, and he had just about enough to cope with. He'd see to those in the morning. He'd kill them off himself if no one else would do it. At the moment all that concerned him was getting to sleep. He heard footsteps up the centre of the ward. McPherson must be back, and he fancied that there was blood on his hands. He sat up in bed and called him over. McPherson came to tuck in his sheets. He looked pale. Although such outbreaks occurred with monotonous regularity, especially in Norman's ward, it was, for McPherson, always the first time. 'Go to sleep, Norman,' he said.

'I can't. Can I have a sleeping-pill?'

'I'll get you one,' McPherson whispered. As he left the bed, the other men sat up and made the same request, calling after him for oblivion. They sat staring until he returned. Then he doled them out, moving from bed to bed, bidding them sleep, forcing a little gruffness into his voice. He didn't want any of them to think he was getting soft. 'Is he all right, Billy?' Norman asked, when McPherson reached his bed.

'He'll be all right,' McPherson said. 'He'll be back. He's got a lampshade to finish, or his mother'll have something to say about that.' He winked at Norman. 'Go to sleep,' he said. 'Everything looks better in the morning.'

He left the bed, and Norman shut his eyes quickly. He knew they were there, and what's more, they would be there in the morning, too. Everything is not better in the morning. They would be there and Billy would be gone. He would have been glad not to wake up at all. But in order not to wake, he had to go to sleep. He buried his hand in the pillow, but withdrew it quickly, knowing they were there too. He felt a drowsiness coming over him, and he surrendered with a coward's gratitude. Soon the ward was silent and Minister turned over in his sleep and groaned, as if he had had a bad dream.

13

Apart from breaks for feeding, Minister was not woken the following day, and Norman panicked. He had come to the end of his supply, and the things were crawling over the wall and over his body. He waited until after breakfast. It was a fine day, and most of the patients, except those who slept and had slept ever since Norman had arrived, had gone out on to the lawns, to read or write letters, or play chess, or simply to beg the day to swallow them whole. The ward was quiet, and the nurse-in-charge was in the outside corridor. Norman went over to Minister's bed. He looked at him and resented his healthy countenance. 'Minister,' he whispered. He gave him a slight shove. He had to test how much it would need to wake Minister up. Minister didn't move. The rhythm of his slight snore did not change. Norman tapped him sharply on the rump, but that too, made little impression. For a moment, Norman thought of the consequences of beating him blue and awake, but he didn't care. His panic had bred hatred. He threw his body with all its force on to the heap of Minister. 'Wake up, you bastard,' he hissed. 'Wake up, or I'll kill you.'

Minister turned over and opened an offended eye. 'What, what?' he groaned. Norman heard the nurse behind him. 'Nothing,' he said, 'I tripped. Sorry.' He slunk away from the bed, and lay down on his own. He didn't know what to do. He had been without pills before, and he remembered the excruciating pains of withdrawal. If he lay there long enough, or even if he were up and moving, they would overrun his helpless body and how could he explain these sudden pains to the nurses. And supposing nobody believed he was in pain. He opened his eyes. He had to. When they were closed, his head swam in nausea. But when they were open he could see them, and there was nowhere he could turn not to see them. Because they were everywhere. On his body too. He dared not scratch on one place, because they would settle somewhere else about him, and his whole body would be seething with their filth. 'It's these bloody sheets,' he said aloud. He sat up on the bed and looked over at Minister. There was no point in trying again. The nurse was hovering in Minister's area. He began to shiver. 'Oh God,' he screamed, 'it's coming, it's coming,' and he ran down to the end of the ward, as if running from the pain. He opened the cleaning cupboard and brought out a huge package of detergent. Then he went along one side of the wall, and haunted with his fears, he sprinkled the powder along the skirting. The nurse came over. 'What d'you think you're doing?' he said. Norman ignored him. The packet was almost empty and he looked back at his trail of blue powder. 'That'll kill the bastards,' he said. The nurse grasped his shoulder. 'What are you doing, Norman?' he said.

'Why can't you fucking well keep this ward clean?' He ran over to his bed and stripped it with a speed and strength that astonished him. He took his pillows and plunged them into the nearest sink and turned the water. 'Drown, you bastards, drown,' he said. He started to gather up other pillows, but the nurse got him from behind.

It was all done very quickly. The second nurse came over and plunged the needle into his arm. Between them, they carried him to his bed. They gave him new pillows and tucked him in like a baby. Then they swept the powder from the floor and took away the sodden linen. By the time the men came back into the ward, they had removed all evidence of Norman's turning, and Norman had joined Minister in a colourless and painless limbo.

They kept him asleep for a fortnight, till they got the poison out of him. Awakened for meals, he ate drowsily, with no notion of what he was consuming. Occasionally he saw the bewildered face of his father, and Bella kept touching him. He heard voices and preferred not to think they were addressed to him. Where did you get them from? Who gave, who gave, tell me, tell me, who gave? That must have been his father. But he slept it all away. Towards the end, they dosed him less heavily, and he was able to sit up in bed, and to register the fact that Minister was gone.

They got him up, and walked him round the ward and out

into the gardens. He was glad to admit to feeling better, but he suffered too, a terrible sense of loss. Coupled with this was his remorse which painfully manifested itself when his father and Bella came to see him. 'I'm sorry,' was all he could say, 'I'm sorry for everything I've done to you.' He did not plead any more to be taken home. He felt much too inadequate and deservedly unwanted, to merit that kind of request. Rabbi Zweck, overjoyed by his son's recovery, tried to ignore the doctor's warning that it might not last. 'We still have to find out *why* he wants pills,' the doctor said. 'Only when we've sorted that one out, can we be hopeful that he won't go back on them.' Rabbi Zweck was prepared to be patient, but what pained him more than anything else, was his son's penitence. 'No need to be sorry,' he said to him. 'Is not your fault. Now we forget everything. We start again. You get better, you come home. You go back to the Law, and we start again.'

For Rabbi Zweck, it was suddenly as if nothing had interrupted his son's brilliant career. The fiasco of his last appearance at the Bar, and his subsequent breakdowns were episodes of a nightmare that would never recur, and like a nightmare, deniable. 'You remember, Norman, the Watson case?' he said. 'You remember, Bella?' He wanted to gather her into her brother's past triumph. He wanted to realize it into the present, as if even now, the newspapers were singing his praises, and the clients were flocking to his door.

'Nobody thought he'd get off,' Bella said. 'What did he get? Three years, was it, for manslaughter? He'll be out pretty soon.'

'No,' Rabbi Zweck said quickly. He was angry that Bella had so squarely placed her brother's success in the distant past, as if it were over and done with, and could never occur again. 'Not so long ago it was, Norman,' he said. He was anxious to re-tell the tale, so that it would live again, and rekindle for Norman the elation of his success. 'What was it now? I forget already,' he said, looking at Bella urging her to re-cap the tale for them all to savour. 'Was it a bread-knife he used?' He giggled, embarrassed by his fragmented memory. All that was vivid in his mind, was the aftermath of the case, the adulation that his son had received, and his own unbounded pleasure.

'You made out that it was self-defence,' Bella was saying. 'It wasn't really though, was it. *You* never believed that, did you, Norman?'

'What does it matter what he believes?' Rabbi Zweck interrupted. He could see the danger in that question. 'With another lawyer, hanged he would have been, that murderer. That's what they all said. He'll hang, they said, so cocksure they all were. Well, they didn't reckon with Norman Zweck,' he said proudly. 'In the court, all those clever people, suddenly they're crying for the murderer, with Norman speaking about the terrible life with his terrible wife the murderer was having. I also wept a little. And you remember after the sentence how they all cheered. Such a hooray there was. And all because of Norman Zweck,' he said, thrusting his face close to his son's. He grasped Norman's hand. 'He owes his life to you, that murderer. Who should deny it? And how they all came running afterwards. All the murderers. All the thieves. Suddenly, everybody wanted Zweck. You remember, Norman?' he whispered. 'And now again, they'll want you. You go back to the Law and we start again.'

Norman took his hand away, and hid his face in the pillow.

Perhaps he should not have mentioned the Law bit, Rabbi Zweck thought. In all honesty, it was what *he*, his father wanted him to do, and Rabbi Zweck knew by instinct, that his expectations and hopes for Norman had contributed in large measure to his son's breakdown. 'Is Norman must lead Norman's life,' he kept saying to himself, and he recalled Minister's remark on his first visit to the hospital, oh, how many long weeks ago? 'When I die,' he'd said, 'it won't be my death at all. Like my life, it'll be something that happened to my Mum.' It was as if all had been clarified, and that Norman's sojourn in hospital was a lesson primarily for his father.

A few days after Norman's deep sleep, the doctors decided that he was ready for intensive treatment. He was depressed which was to be expected but he was not silent. He talked endlessly to the nurses and the other patients. He had no curiosity about anyone else's condition; his concern with his own was supreme, and he talked about his problems endlessly. At first, he made an erratic start with his doctor. He wanted to tell everything, as if it would elude him and embed itself behind his mind, and take yet another spell of pain and hallucination before it would risk showing itself again. Over the weeks, he calmed down, but every session reverted to 'her', whose name stuck in his throat. No matter what the subject, it was always Esther who dodged through the cluttered events of his life, nagging to be heard. So it marked a decisive advance in Norman's analysis when, after a few weeks, overcome by an oppressive melancholy, he was able, tentatively, to speak about her.

Dr Littlestone was smoking a pipe when Norman came into the room. It was a smell to which Norman had at other times been indifferent, but today, possibly because of his acute depression, the fumes nauseated him. He begged the doctor with almost servile deference, to put it out. The doctor obliged, but the fumes still hung in the air. Norman went to the window and opened it. Then he sat down, waiting for the smell to subside. They waited in silence. Then, after a few minutes, the doctor went to the window. 'Shall I shut it now?' he asked.

Norman nodded.

Dr Littlestone shut the window and sat on the corner of his desk. 'How are you Norman?' he said. It marked the regular opening of a session. It was not a question that required an answer. It meant, simply, 'Let's go on from where we left off.'

'I must tell you about her,' Norman blurted out. 'I must tell you about my ... er ... sister.'

Dr Littlestone moved over to his chair, and sat down. Norman's opening promised a fruitful session.

After his initial announcement, Norman did not know how to carry on. He sought for a beginning, but all that crowded into his mind, was the final denouement of disaster. He could have started at the end and worked his way backward, until a beginning would have found itself, simply when he would stop talking. But, depressed as he was, he still had a feeling for shape, drama and climax, a hangover from his barrister training. 'She,' he began, 'my sister ...'

Dr Littlestone waited. He didn't want to give any help at this stage. Norman was articulate enough. Once he got started, he would gather his own momentum. He doodled idly on his pad, and then, without thinking, he put the pad away. The gesture

gave Norman confidence. The pad reminded him of the policeman's note-book, in which I ought to warn you that anything
you say will be taken down and may be used in evidence against
you. Norman wanted to get his story out, but he wanted it
forgotten, he never wanted it to be referred to again. 'People
used to think she was pretty,' he began. It helped, he found, to
distance her, to give other people the responsibility for her
story. 'They thought she was pretty,' he repeated, 'but I myself
never took much notice of her. Not until David started to look
at her. When she was about . . .' He paused, dissatisfied with the
shape the story was taking. 'I suppose I should tell you about
David,' he said. 'It's really about David I've got to tell you.'

'Who is David?' Dr Littlestone said. He didn't remember
hearing the name. If Norman had ever mentioned it, it was in
passing, and without any significance.

'David was . . .' Norman hesitated. He fumbled with the fold
of his dressing-gown. 'Nothing, nothing,' he said aggressively.
'He was my friend, that's all.'

'Tell me about Esther then.'

Norman shrugged helplessly. His mouth was full of vocabulary, yet there seemed no way to distil it in any kind of order.
He let his mind wander away from the whole sorry story. He
thought of Minister. He missed him. He must have been discharged when Norman was in his deep sleep. He wished he
could contact him again. What point was there in living this so-
called sane way of life, when all zest was drained out of him,
and all he was left with was a clear recognition of his own
torment that hammered at his skull. He could have done without such memories to nag at him. He had kept them dormant
and controlled in his white days. On reflection, the silver-fish
were preferable to any thought of David. He knew it was wrong
to wish anyone into the hell-hole, but he hoped that Minister
would come back and push David out of his mind once more.

Dr Littlestone twiddled his pencil. 'You were going to tell me
about Esther,' he said softly.

'It doesn't matter.'

'Are you very fond of her?' he said.

'I hate her. Can't you see that? I hate her and I'll never see
her again.'

'When did you start hating her?'

'I don't remember. Always, I suppose. I hope I did, anyway. Whatever's wrong with me, she started it all. She's hateable, she's rotten.'

'How was it her fault?'

'She didn't have to do it, did she?'

'It depends on what she did.'

'She left him, that's what she did. She didn't have to do that, did she?'

'It depends on her reasons.'

'Oh, let's forget it,' Norman said. He didn't want to discuss it, so that someone else could take his sister's side. There was no defence for her anyway. He just wanted to tell the story without any interruption, and especially without comments of partiality. 'Let's forget it,' he said again.

'Would you like to go back into the ward? I'll be seeing you again at the end of the week. Perhaps it'll be easier then.'

'No, I don't want to go back. It'll only nag at me.' He leaned on the desk and put his head in his hands.

'Don't worry about the order of things,' Dr Littlestone said. 'Try to make a start. Anywhere.'

Norman lifted his head. 'We were in *shul* one day,' he began softly, though as he knew, not at the beginning, 'and I saw him looking at her.'

'Who were you with?' Dr Littlestone asked, putting his pencil down, 'and who was she that he was looking at?'

'I was with David,' Norman went on, slightly irritated by the interruption, 'and she was ... well she was my sister. She was upstairs. You know they separate us in *shul*. The women sit upstairs and the men down below. We used to spend most of our time looking up and seeing them come in. It was more noticeable when we did it, more noticeable than when they did it, that is. Because the centre of our attention was supposed to be downstairs anyway, where my father was standing. At that time, he was Minister of the Congregation.' Minister, Norman thought, and it was the first time he'd connected that connotation with his erstwhile pusher. 'Yes, he was the minister there in those days,' he said aloud. 'We used to spend most of our time looking upwards, David and I. I think most Jewish marriages begin like that, looking upwards. It's an enforced kind of idolatry. Maybe that was the point of the separation. I don't know. Anyway, that's how we used to spend our time in *shul*.' He paused. 'What was I saying?' he said.

'You're in the synagogue,' Dr Littlestone said. 'You're with David, and Esther's upstairs.'

'Yes, that's right. And he was looking at her. I caught him looking at her and when he saw me looking at him, he blushed a little, as if he were guilty. Then I thought to myself, how long has this been going on? And I was angry, for two reasons. First, that I hadn't noticed it, and second, that it was going on at all.'

'Why should you be angry about it?' Dr Littlestone asked.

'I was jealous, I suppose. After a while, when they really got going together, I was glad about it. I was very happy about it in fact. But in the beginning I was jealous, because, well, he was my best friend. I wanted him all to myself. He was my only friend, in fact, I couldn't afford to share him.'

'Tell me about your friendship,' Dr Littlestone said.

Norman left off fiddling with the folds of his dressing-gown. He leaned back in the chair. He was feeling less depressed, already slightly detached from the story. 'How do you describe a friendship?' he said, as if the two of them were engaged in a philosophical encounter. 'In hindsight I can examine it, and ascribe this meaning to it, or that. But at the time, I didn't know what it was all about. All I knew was that I was happy when I was with him, that he was part of me, as I was of him. That we fought like two brothers, and loved likewise. I loved him more than that, I think.' Norman fiddled with his dressing-gown again. 'Well, maybe,' he shrugged. He was depressed again, and the detachment was gone. 'Once I went away to stay with my aunt for a week, and I couldn't stand it. Nothing to do with my aunt. It was him. I missed him and I worried about who he was with and what he was doing. I had to stick the week out, hiding my feelings, 'cos I knew, even then, that there was something unnatural about them. Then when I came back, he was waiting for me in my house, and his mother was there, and she said, well thank God you're back. He's been sulking the whole week. Such aggravation I've had from him. She was like my mother.

She was always having aggravation. And not just aggravation. *Such* aggravation they were always having. We never aggravated them. They never found us aggravating. It was only that we gave them such aggravation. We gave it to them when we came home late from school, when we didn't wash our hands before a meal, when our shoelaces were undone. Throughout our childhood, it seems the only thing we gave our mothers was aggravation. And not just aggravation, but *such* aggravation. I used to think aggravation was a yiddish word.' He smiled to himself, remembering the joy of that homecoming and the knowledge that David had missed him equally. He looked up at Dr Littlestone. 'Well, that's the kind of friends we were,' he said.

'Were your mothers friendly?'

Norman did not see the relevance of the question, and he answered with little interest. 'Yes, I suppose they were. They were always together. She made our clothes. My mother was always being measured for something. David didn't have a father you see. He died when David was a baby. It was our local tragedy. We grew up with the story. We didn't know how he died; there was a feeling abroad that we shouldn't ask. It became a kind of myth. That's why she didn't marry again I suppose. It would have been letting down one of our local traditions. She was a "good woman" as they called her, bringing him up on her own, and earning a living as a dressmaker. Yes, they were good friends, she and my mother.'

'Were you orthodox, you and David. Did you go to the synagogue every Saturday?'

Norman laughed. 'Oh, the *shul* was only the smallest part of it. Yes, we were religious all right. It's pretty difficult not to be, if your father's a minister. We went every Friday night too. And we used to go to *cheder* together. That's our Sunday school, and my father would teach us privately too. My father felt responsible for David's Jewish education, since he didn't have a father of his own. Yes, we were orthodox all right.'

He fiddled with his dressing-gown cord again. He found it difficult to keep his mind on the story. He kept thinking of Minister. What right had he to be discharged without leaving any provision for his clients? He wondered if others in the ward depended upon him, but on the whole, unless it was obvious what was the matter with them, the men didn't volunteer why they were there. So there was no way of knowing who was suffering from Minister's absence. Who wasn't suffering, Norman thought. They were all in hell here, anyway. And here was he just scratching at the surface of his story that was pleading in the pit of his stomach for release. He wanted Dr Littlestone's help and yet he resented his every question. He wanted to tell the story on his own, in his own way, and keep it to himself, and not to donate it as a mere case-history. Because, like his dreams, whomever they were about, they, like his story, were his and nobody else's.

Dr Littlestone coughed to affirm his presence. 'In the beginning,' he said, 'you wanted to tell me about Esther. Tell me about her before David happened.'

'There never was a time when David hadn't happened. At least, I don't remember it. And if there was, it wouldn't have been of any importance.'

Dr Littlestone leaned back in his chair. He shoved his legs forward and made almost a production of making himself comfortable. For the first time in the session, he looked as if he wanted to listen, not for any professional purpose, but out of sheer untrammelled interest. And Norman responded. He started, painfully at first, but gathered momentum as the story took hold. As he began, he had a fleeting awareness that he was about to destroy what was his strongest defence, and an accompanying fear of what he could build to replace it. Would the white days come back, and were they dependent on the story or was it the other way around. But it was unfolding itself, almost without his volition, the story of Esther and what it had done to him.

'Esther was around a long time before I took much notice of her. She was the baby, and everyone spoilt her. She was pretty too, with the kind of prettiness that didn't run in our family. Well, take a look at me, for instance, and my sister Bella's not so hot, either. You've seen her when she visits me. My mother was no beauty, and my father, well, I've never considered him in those terms. Anyway, Esther was pretty, you couldn't deny it, and as she grew older she even became beautiful. It worried my father a bit, because he thought it would go to her head, so he spent more time on Esther's education, the Jewish side of it, I mean, than he did on me or Bella. He loved her too, to distraction, and so did my mother, but I'm not blaming Esther for that. She was the baby and she was pretty and neither of those facts was her fault. But I suppose they were afraid that her beauty would tempt her into a wider world than we were supposed to enter, the world of the goyim, as my parents called it. But as a result of my father's dedication, Esther became more religious than all of us. She was always looking for new rules in the Law to obey. It used to irritate me. Above all, I used to find it priggish, but we weren't allowed to say a word against her. Well, she grew up, and she didn't interfere with me in any way, and David was around most of the time, and neither of us had time for anybody else. I noticed sometimes that she was pretty horrible to my sister Bella. She used to make fun of her because she was grown up and still wore little white socks. I don't know why Bella did it, but they were her feet after all, and she was entitled to put what she liked on them. Anyway, that's another story and it's got nothing to do with me.'

Dr Littlestone shifted in his chair. 'It's got nothing to do with me, those white socks,' he repeated. 'That's Bella's problem, and it's me who's in this place, so forget it. It's Esther I'm telling you about.'

'I'm listening,' Dr Littlestone said.

'Well, when she was fifteen, she left school. Apart from Hebrew and Jewish learning and that sort of thing, she wasn't very bright. For a while she helped in the shop. We've got a grocer shop, you know,' he said. 'We live above it. It was my mother's, and she used to run it when my father was congregational minister. Then, when my father retired, he went into the shop and they shared the work between them. Well, the shop wasn't really busy enough to warrant all those assistants, especially since a supermarket had opened down the road, so Esther left and took over some of my father's Hebrew classes. The young ones, at first, then gradually, after a few years, she took over the entire *cheder*. My parents were proud of her. At the time, I had just qualified and I was beginning to make a modest living. They were proud of me too. In fact, when I think about it, they had plenty to be happy about. There was Bella, of course, getting older and less marriageable, but every Jewish family has a Bella. They're a kind of *nachus* too. Too bad on the Bellas of course, but she seemed reasonably content, though those white socks of hers were beginning to get me down too. It's all a bit confusing, isn't it?' he said.

He wondered what Dr Littlestone was making of it all, but in fact he didn't really care. He didn't even care whether he found the story interesting. What was important was that the story should be told. Not even he was interested in the story any more which probably accounted for the dull fluency of its telling. It was as if he were relating the facts to a court of law, as if it had all happened to somebody else, and for some reason Norman had become the catalyst to pass it on. 'I made lots of new friends in my job,' he continued, 'but it was David who remained my closest, and I would rush home from work to spend the evening with him, or to sit with him while he studied. He was in his last year of medicine. I used to sit with him in his room and watch him at his desk. His head always rested on his left hand, but he didn't stoop over the books. Even as he worked he was upright, and his face reflected the excitement of what he read and wrote. Often he would grasp his hands together when he had ferreted out the core of some problem, and he would try to share the magic of his discovery with me. He would explain it carefully and as patiently as he could. He was one of the few people I had ever met who was genuinely excited by knowledge. When he put his books away, I would tell him about my day. He'd ask me endless questions. He wanted to know every detail of the case I was working on, and he was infinitely moved by the Law's inadequacies and the wretchedness of those who came into contact with it. Occasionally, if he could take off the time, he would come to court. I would wait for him to turn up in the public gallery and I would save my oratory for him. Now I recollect it,' Norman said, almost to himself, 'I think I have never been happier in my whole life. When he qualified, we celebrated together, just the two of us, in his room. We talked, I don't know what about. All I remember was my joy at his success, and his joy that he could share it.'

Norman looked across the desk and seemed surprised that Dr Littlestone was staring at him. For the past few minutes he had been talking, he felt, almost to himself, and seeing Dr Littlestone there, he remembered the object of the whole session. 'I'm coming to Esther,' he promised. 'It's just that I'm happier talking about him.' He sighed with the weariness of having to get on with the job. 'Well,' he went on, 'it was a long time before all this that the Esther business started, before David qualified, and my father was still a minister. We got back from *shul* that day, and I tackled him. I asked him what there was between him and my sister. He was absolutely honest with me, and surprised and a little hurt, I think, that I was angry. He told me that he had a very special feeling for her, that he would like to go out with her, that he hadn't yet asked her, but that he was going to. He made that quite clear. We quarrelled. I was stupid. Even at the time I knew it. I went home and sulked. And naturally, while I was sulking, and refusing to go and see him, the thing took its course. He used to come over to the house and I avoided him, and Esther's obvious happiness made me squirm.

'I suppose I enjoyed my misery for a while. Whenever he tried to approach me, I brushed him off. I liked doing it. I wanted to provoke a precarious rift between us, so that our reconciliation could be that much more beautiful. They began to talk of an engagement, and marriage as soon as he qualified. Then, when it seemed a *fait accompli*, I got tired of the role I was playing. I missed him terribly, and it seemed that Esther would have to become part of us. So we made it up. Our reconciliation was not nearly as exciting as I had anticipated. I had sulked for too long. But we were still close. In fact, as far as he was concerned, I had the impression that his feelings towards me were intensified. We still saw each other alone. He wanted Esther to make no difference to our friendship. This pleased me too; we had a kind of exclusive relationship that nobody, not even Esther, could even begin to understand. He didn't talk about her, but I could see that they were very much in love, and I grew to be happy for both of them. He worked hard for his finals while my mother and his made plans for the wedding.

'Then suddenly something happened to Esther. I don't suppose it was sudden. It must have gone on for some time, but I didn't notice it. Her face changed. I noticed it one morning at breakfast. It's hard to describe what had happened. All the features were exactly the same as before. It was the ensemble that had changed. She looked older somehow, sadder, and even more beautiful. She was quiet and suddenly introspective. My mother ascribed her moods to love; my father said nothing, but I was worried. Often she would try and talk to me alone, but I avoided her. I suspected she wanted to discuss David with me, and I couldn't risk the jealousy that would ensue. Something was happening to her that was outside us all. She saw David daily as before, but I noticed that she avoided being alone with him. She wouldn't go out; she wanted to stay home with him and the family every evening. It was the summer holiday and there was no Hebrew school. Esther spent her day times working at her studies in the library. There was nothing untoward about that, yet sometimes I thought she spent an inordinate time there. Once I happened to pass her bedroom, and I saw her staring into the mirror. She had tied her hair back and tucked it tightly into a scarf. Esther had intended to shave her head when she married in accordance with the Jewish law, and possibly she was trying out what it would look like. I thought perhaps it worried her and that was why she had changed. I felt a threat in the house – perhaps this is hindsight, I don't know – but I definitely remember an unaccountable fear that no one else in the house seemed to share.

'Then one night, it was a Sunday towards the end of the summer, we were sitting at home, that is Bella, me and my parents. David had gone to his uncle's and Esther was out with an old school friend. My mother was knitting, I remember, and my father was reading in the prayer book. Bella was reading too. I was doing some preliminary work on a case. We were all busy and it was my mother who first noticed the time. It was past midnight and Esther was not home. It was raining, and my father's immediate concern was whether she'd taken a mackintosh and he sent Bella to Esther's room to look in her wardrobe. After a few minutes, Bella came back white-faced, holding a letter. "I found this on the bed," she said.

'On the envelope, Esther had written, "To the family", but none of us at that moment were anxious for membership. She

139

put it on the kitchen-table and it lay there, an object of terror.
"You read it," my mother and father said together. Bella was
reluctant to pick the letter up. Often if it's bad news, as the
letter obviously was, it's the teller who takes the blame, and
neither Bella nor I wanted that. Yet we both reached for it at
the same time, each wanting to save the other from blame. We
were very close at that moment, with the kind of closeness
families achieve when one of their members dies. "I'll read it,"
we said together, and then I took the letter from her and I
opened it. "I knew it, I knew it," my mother was crying, and all
of us guessed what she knew. I only had to confirm it in my
reading. I remember it by heart, though I only read the letter
that one time, but each word seared me fourfold, for myself
and the others around the table. "Dear my family," it said, and
I remember the grammar offending me, "You will be shocked to
read this letter, but I cannot hold the truth from you any
longer. Two weeks ago I was married." I was afraid to look at
my parents, but I heard my mother scream. My father uttered a
shrivelled moan, and started, as if automatically, to turn the
pages of the prayer book he was reading. "Go on, go on," Bella
said, hoping for some kind of denial in the next sentence. I went
back to the letter. "I've married John," it said. "I have been
seeing him for many months, and I couldn't fight it. I love him
very much, and we are very happy." '

Norman looked at Dr Littlestone. 'This John,' he spat the
name, 'he was the librarian in the local library. Friend of the
family for years. In fact, our only non-Jewish friend. He used
to keep books back for me. He sometimes came to the house
when David was there. He used to bring books for my father.
He took some kind of lurid interest in Jewish things. Yes, where
was I? Yes, "I love him very much and we are very happy. I
have written to David, but please help to explain it all to him."
After the mention of David, I lost interest in what had happened to her. I finished reading the letter that asked for our
forgiveness, and I saw my parents' pain, but I thought only of
David, and I must admit, with a certain excitement, as to how I
would comfort him. I wanted to get out of the house, but David
was away and I had to sit there and see their torment. My
mother's screams had subsided; now there was a deep con-

tinuous moan, that racked her body with animal pain. She swayed to and fro, wailing and shivering with the horror of the news. I heard my father mumble, and when I dared to look at him, I saw that he had turned the pages of the book to the Prayers for the Dead.'

Norman shivered. He realized that he had forgotten that last incident. Suddenly, he wanted to be with his father, to go home and to love him. It was the safest thing any man could do, he thought, just to love and care for somebody. It wasn't a happy thing, it wasn't even a justifiable thing to love, it was safe, that's all it was, and he longed to give himself just that kind of security. 'Poor Pop,' he said to himself. He stared out of the window. Poor everybody, in fact, and the misery of all their lives, Bella, his parents, and David's came to overwhelm him. 'And David,' he said softly. 'I waited till the following day. I was going to see him in the evening after my work. He would have read Esther's letter by then, and the whole day, I rehearsed to myself how I would help him. I was excited as I reached his room, and I remember feeling that it was wrong to be so excited. I called his name as I climbed the stairs. I always did that, so that by the time I got to his door, he would be expecting me. He didn't answer, but I went in anyway. At least, I tried to get in. His door opened about six inches, then it seemed to be blocked. As I pushed the door open, I felt myself sweating, and I knew as my mother had known before I had opened the letter.

'There's not much more,' Norman said in a sudden matter-of-fact voice. 'He was on the bed dead from the bleeding. He was so soaked in his death, that it was impossible to tell where it first sprouted.' Norman paused. His eyes were burning with dryness, and he wished that he could cry. 'I went to his funeral,' he said. 'Because he was a suicide, they buried him against the wall. And no one was allowed to mourn for him, but on the quiet I sat on a low stool, because I'd lost a brother. That's all,' he said quickly. 'That's all I had to tell you.'

He got up. He was afraid that Dr Littlestone might say something and he was in no mood for another's opinion. He was acutely disappointed with the whole session. He had pinned so much hope on getting the story out and it had left him sadder than he had been when he rolled agonized down David's stairs.

The pain, as now, was physical and exhausting. He went to the door. As he opened it he turned and saw Dr Littlestone, not as the listener he had been, but in his white-coated function, his pad and pen within his grasp, and he was swept with a loathing for him for having received his confidence. 'And if you're in the least bit interested,' he said, with a contempt that crept reluctantly into his voice, 'if you're interested, it was then that I started on the pills. I'd been offered them before, of course, but this time, I took them.'

He closed the door, and went down the corridor to the ward. He slouched close to the wall, bent with his melancholy. He'd often experienced a dream to be more disturbing than the reality, and he felt the same kind of disturbance after telling his story. What's the good, he thought? I've told him about David, and there's really nothing more to tell about anything, yet I feel as I feel and I shall be in this place for ever. He walked through the swing doors. At the end of the ward he saw a group of men. Someone stood in the centre, and they seemed to be listening with avid interest to his story. One of them turned at the noise of the doors. 'Look who's back, Norman,' he shouted. He stepped aside so that Norman could see through the circle. In its centre was Minister. Pyjamaed, and back in harness. It was as if David had not died at all. Norman rushed up to him, and Minister opened his arms. 'I know what *you* want, mate,' he whispered in his ear. ' 'Ow you been going in my absence then?'

'Oh, thank God you're back,' Norman said. 'I missed you. Where have you been?'

'I was called to a Cabinet meeting,' he said.

The other men laughed nervously, afraid to mock him, yet equally afraid to take him seriously.

'Called in on my Mum on the way from Parliament,' Minister was saying, 'and I found a man in Mum's bed. " 'Ullo, 'ullo," I said, "and what are you doing in Mum's bed?" "I'm your new Dad son," he said, and I said to meself, this lot isn't for you, lad, so I upped and come back to the office.' The men laughed, with a little more confidence this time; madness became acceptable if it were mad enough, and if it went on for long enough, and it was as if Minister had never left the ward. He went over to his old bed and Norman followed him.

'Prices have gone up a bit,' he said over his shoulder. 'Cost of living and all that. Been doing a bit of studying while I was away. I told them in the Cabinet. Pills, I said, is essential like soap. They sat there scratching themselves like they never used soap neither. You can't tell 'em anything. Soap's gone up, too, on the outside. So 'as everything else. My mum sends you 'er love,' he said irrelevantly, 'and you can 'ave it, as far as I'm concerned, every rotten drop of it. She's got soap all right. Scrubbing the bloody place from morning till night, and there's cowpads up to your knees. Two pounds a day they've gone up to,' he said without a pause, 'but as many as you like. I bought a job lot, 'olesale. Where's Billy?'

'He'll come back,' Norman said, 'like you came back. Like I'll come back,' he said to himself, 'if I ever get away. Can I have some now, Minister?' Norman said. 'I've got the money.'

'Tomorrow,' Minister said, as he turned back the bedclothes. 'Tomorrow, you'n me'll make a fresh start. White for breakfast, mate?'

Now they were within his reach, he was impatient. 'I've got to have them,' he said, and he even felt a twinge of withdrawal pain.

'Tomorrow,' Minister said with finality, and he crouched down between the sheets. 'Must get my beauty sleep,' he said.

Norman looked at him lying there. What hell was his outside, that he should be happy to return to a place like this. Or had they forced him back, lying at the back of a handle-less car, his body pinned by a welfare boot. He went over to his bed. The prospect of a white tomorrow heartened him. If David could not die in him of his own accord, when he had given him every chance, then he would have to whiten him into oblivion.

14

Rabbi Zweck no longer had the nagging urge to ransack Norman's room for clues. After the fiasco of the whore's address, he was reluctant to follow up any more of his findings. Yet he went into the room occasionally to sit on the bed, to keep it warm, as it were, against his son's return. As the weeks passed, the nightmare of Norman's detention faded. He went to see him once or twice a week, and sometimes Bella would go on her own. Norman had stopped nagging to come home, and apart from the period of his deep sleep, the visits were less disturbing. Sometimes it frightened Rabbi Zweck that he had found the situation so acceptable. He wondered what had happened to Billy. A few weeks ago he had been to the hospital, and Billy's bed was empty. Norman said he didn't know where Billy was, and nobody else would volunteer any information. Rabbi Zweck had hoped that Billy had gone home. But when the next day, as he was walking to the bus-stop after his visit, he saw Billy's father and mother waiting there, he lagged behind and waited for the next bus, because he could not bear to face them after his hopes for their boy had been shattered. He wondered where Billy was incarcerated. He half-knew, but he tried not to think about it. He worried about Billy as much as he did about Norman. Somehow, he saw them doomed or saved together.

During the past few weeks, while Norman had been away, he had grown very close to Bella. And he had noticed a reciprocal gentleness from her. There was often laughter in the house between them. It was like in the old days, when Sarah was alive, and Esther was home and Norman was well. Lately, too, since Norman's departure, he had thought more often of Esther, and with less bitterness. Secretly he often wished he could see her again, and it was largely out of respect for Sarah's memory that he had never asked her to come home. Esther's marriage had broken Sarah. It had not caused her death. No one dies of a broken heart. But the cancer that carried her off, did so obligingly, because Sarah had begun to die the moment she had seen Esther's letter. A child, Esther was, only seventeen, and almost twenty years ago. Had the marriage lasted that long, and could she possibly be happy, without even a child to hold it together? He wondered whether he should write to her. He knew Bella kept in touch with her and he was grateful for that. Perhaps he could offer to add a line to her next letter. He wondered whether she knew about Norman, and whether she wanted to come and see him. He made up his mind to write to her. She was entitled after all to know about her brother, but almost at the same moment, he decided against it. It would be disloyal to Sarah.

He was restless. He had never been at a loss for something to do. Ever since his retirement from his services to the congregation, his studies of Jewish history and religion had occupied him, and there was always the shop to vary the routine. But they were not busy downstairs, and Bella and the assistant could more than manage on their own. Normally at this hour, he would be reading, but in the last few weeks he had been restless with that too. It was as if everything was pushing to come to a head, and could not ripen without his participation. He didn't know what it was, but there was no doubt that things in the house were changing. Norman's absence, his closeness to Bella, and these constant thoughts of Esther.

He wondered what he could do. He looked about Norman's room, and for the first time, Norman's belongings, his clothes, his books, his dressing-table equipment, seemed out of place, as if they'd been hurriedly stuffed away until the right place had been found for them. Suddenly Rabbi Zweck knew what he had to do. He would remove Norman from Sarah's room, or rather, he would shed Norman of his mother. Rabbi Zweck would return to the marriage bed, and Norman would be freed from his painful inheritance. That would be a good beginning, he thought, for Norman's return.

He was glad he had decided on something, and he got up quickly from the bed, and set to work. As he rose, he felt a twinge in his upper arm, and a gradual pressure around the region of his heart, a pain that had nothing to do with sorrow. It was not the first time he'd felt it. Several times during the past few weeks, he had had the identical sensation. But always the pain passed away. He sat down again to let it take its course. It irritated him, this interference with his intentions. Pain always annoyed him, because it wasted time. He had often thought of his own death, and without any fear, but in the past few weeks, he had tried to put such thoughts out of his mind. He could not afford to die at this juncture, with everything in a state of flux and threatening to come to a head. Which is why he took no notice of his pain. It passed as he sat there, and he allowed it a little extra time. Then he stood up and planned his campaign. He thought it better to carry out the operation simultaneously, that is, to make one journey to his little room with a bundle of Norman's things, and to return with an equal bundle of his own. That way, the rooms would each transform themselves gradually, and in the process, he would become used to his own new status.

He opened the wardrobe, and started on the clothes. Sarah's dresses were still interspersed with Norman's suits. He took them off the rail one by one. One of Sarah's dress sleeves had caught in the pocket of one of Norman's suits, not caught, Rabbi Zweck thought, as he tried to pull it out, but tucked there, as it were, deliberately. It unnerved him, this produced partnership, and more so, when he found it repeated along the line. He pulled the sleeves out of the pockets and was disturbed by his feelings of disgust. 'Ach,' he muttered, 'is time already to separate them.'

He carried a pile of Norman's clothes into his own room, and laid them on the bed. Then he collected his own for the return journey. The process took him most of the morning. He removed Norman's clothes, books and papers, taking care not to examine the latter, and he brought back his own in kind. As the transformation took place, he felt easier and more confident in what he was doing. The last things to go were Norman's hairbrush and toilet articles, and when he'd removed these the dressing-table with Sarah's things took on a pleasurable familiarity. He looked in the wardrobe and saw his own clothes, hung together with hers, side by side, and he made a decent division between Sarah's lot and his own. He looked about the room, and felt pleased with himself. It was like a homecoming.

After his morning's exertions, he was tired, and he laid himself on the bed. It was his bed now, as it had been theirs when Sarah was alive, and Norman had his own room, and that was as it should be. A slight twinge in the upper arm again, the thought of Esther and his good Bella, his memory of Sarah, seemed now all related to each other. He closed his eyes, while the pain passed. 'I must take it easy,' he said to himself.

As he lay there, the wardrobe door, which he had not completely shut, swung open, revealing that half which contained Sarah's dresses, and as if a curtain had risen on an old well-loved play, Rabbi Zweck lay back and contemplated his late wife's clothes. He knew they would conjure up memories for him, and for that reason he skipped those that had attended events he would sooner forget. He dwelt on the better dresses, the silks and the flowered, a friend's daughter's wedding, a bar-mitzvah, a share in someone else's happiness. Back and fore along the sleeves his eyes wandered, astonished by their powerful evocation. And each time he skipped the brown lace cuff of a sleeve, at first, unable to find its association, but then, with an increased disturbance at each glance. He couldn't envisage the rest of the dress. The cuff was graphic enough, and he knew that an examination of the whole could not have helped him. He didn't want to remember anyway, so he got up and firmly closed the wardrobe door. Then he lay back on the bed.

He felt a tenseness in his body, and he noticed that for some reason, his right first was clenched. He didn't know when it had happened, but he'd experienced the same kind of tenseness before, and always as a prelude to some unpleasant memory. It was, in a way, a physical safeguard against any emotional reaction that memory would engender, as if he were arming himself in advance. He'd noticed of late, how acute his memory had become. The long forgotten events of his life, and usually those he had wanted to forget, would light his mind, usually sparked off by a small incident, something heard, or something seen, like the clenched fist at his side. He remembered the time when Norman had tried to leave home. Why the fist had reminded him of the incident, he could not fathom, but the logic of it, he knew, would eventually reveal itself.

It was when Norman first started to train for the Law, that it had come to a head. He had been hankering after it during his last year at school, and his parents had fobbed him off. The suggestion that Norman should leave a good home, and go and live God knows where, Mrs Zweck found outrageous. But she expressed no opinion. To have directly opposed him, would have meant that she was actually taking his suggestion seriously, and this was the last thing she wanted him to think. It was a fantastic, ridiculous idea, and she would ignore it. When Norman acknowledged that neither his father nor his mother was taking him seriously, he announced his concrete plans.

'I've found a room,' he said, one day at supper.

Mrs Zweck signalled to her husband and the girls to ignore him, and she gave them each a threatening glance which warned them that they would listen to him at their peril. It was her business, and no one else should try to deal with it. 'A little more soup, Abie?' she said.

'I've found a room,' Norman said again.

'Very nice, very nice,' his mother said. 'So little you have to do with your time, you run around to find rooms. Very nice. Very nice.'

'It's a very nice room,' Norman said, mocking her.

'So pleased I am,' she said. 'Such a terrible room you've got in your mother's house, you've got to run look for a nice room. Very nice, very nice,' she said. 'You should enjoy. Now finish your supper,' she suddenly shouted at him. 'Enough already of your jokes.'

'It's not a joke,' he said quietly. 'I'm leaving at the end of the week.'

'Go, go,' she screamed. 'Who's stopping? *I* should stop you? You had enough from your mother? Go. You want I should break my heart? You want you should break up the family?' She challenged the others with her eyes. 'Then go,' she shouted. 'Go.'

'I'd like to go with your blessing,' he said. 'It's not unnatural after all, is it, Pop,' he appealed to his more liberal father, 'that a boy my age should want to leave home.'

'Blessings he wants,' Mrs Zweck was beside herself. 'Not enough he should break the family. I should give him a blessing too. Look, my boy,' she wagged her finger at him, 'I don't want to hear any more about rooms. That's the end of it. You'll stay in this house, you hear me? Until, please God, you get married. Then I won't keep you,' she said generously. 'Then you make your own home, and plenty blessings. Now enough.'

Esther and Bella had been quiet throughout. Even if they had opinions, they knew better than to voice them. Bella instinctively and illogically sided with her mother. She was growing, by force of circumstances, into the role of family protector, and when Norman threatened her parents' peace, she would oppose him, no matter how strong his case. Esther did not have such acute filial feelings. She had been so overloved and protected all her life, that they had never occurred to her. She saw no reason why Norman shouldn't leave home. She for one would be glad to have him gone. He fed and bred her parents' anxiety and love to sickening point, and the house would be happier without him. Every night her mother stood over him as he did his homework, though she understood nothing of the work. She checked and rechecked that all was done, and she had to take his word for it that it was done correctly. She wouldn't dream of going to bed until he came home, and each morning she walked with him to the bus-stop, never failing after all his eighteen years to warn him to be careful as he crossed the road. She could not for one moment believe that his life could be lived without her sanction. He was not an individual, but an appendage of herself. It was no wonder that she employed everything she had against his going.

Rabbi Zweck saw the logic of Norman's wish, and, left alone, he probably would have opposed it on principle at first, and then, with fine argument, given in. But he knew how it would break Sarah and he was too weak to gainsay her. As for Norman, there were only a few moments, like the last, of absolute decision, and yet, even then, it was probably more of a provocation than a declaration of intent. He knew he had to get out of there. His mother had smothered him long enough. Yet he was frightened, not so much of being on his own, but of what his leaving might do to the family. His mother had promised often enough over the past few months that if he went it would be the end of them all, and he could not wholly cast this possibility aside. Besides, there was David. He would probably see less of him, but perhaps that wouldn't be such a bad idea. His closeness to his friend sometimes worried him.

'And what about David, then?' his mother suddenly said, not satisfied to have already had the last word. 'How you going to live without *him*?' she said, and her tone suggested that she knew more of the relationship than Norman did himself. 'Or perhaps you will have a nice little room together?' she sneered.

'Enough, enough,' Rabbi Zweck muttered, 'let's eat in peace.'

So they finished the meal in silence, though Mrs Zweck demonstrated with histrionic gestures, that she'd gone quite off her food. And then in case she had not made her position clear, she announced that she had to lie down.

For a few weeks, the matter was dropped. The summer holidays came and it seemed that Norman had given up his resolution. In fact, the silence that now attended the subject worried Mrs Zweck even more than its discussion. She feared that Norman would move out without a word. Every day when he was out she would go to his room and look for signs of removal. She read his letters in case a clue could be found there, but she found nothing untoward in his belongings. So she made him new curtains for his room, and bought him a new reading-lamp and put up with his sullen silences. But they nagged at her, and fearing that it would all have happened before she could intercede, she brought up the subject again.

'How is the nice rooms?' she said one evening, as they sat in the kitchen together. Rabbi Zweck tried to silence her.

'Momma,' Bella said, 'why don't you leave well alone?'

'What's well about it?' Norman said. 'There's nothing well about my staying here. If you were interested in my room, I'd tell you about it. But you're all completely indifferent.'

Mrs Zweck exploded. 'What room?' she shouted. 'You got another room already?'

'I told you, Momma,' he said patiently, 'months ago, I told you I'd got a room, and I'm moving in there next week.' In fact he hadn't decided in himself when he would go. He was frightened and he kept on postponing it. But his mother was pushing him and in a way he was grateful to her.

'Now stop all this nonsense,' Mrs Zweck said. 'There'll be no more argument. You stay in this house.'

Rabbi Zweck looked at his son. He was considerably taller than any of them, and he wondered how his wife intended to keep him there.

'If I hear another word about this room business, I'll ... I'll ...'

'You'll what?' Norman dared to ask her.

But since Mrs Zweck had no idea what she would do, she covered her loss of words with a veiled threat. 'Doesn't matter,' she said. 'You'll see. That's all I'll tell you. You'll see and you'll be sorry. So sorry you'll be.' She left it there and hoped it was having some effect. But though Norman did not take her threats too seriously, he was too dependent on her to dismiss them altogether. He went to his room. Mrs Zweck followed him and listened outside the door. She fully expected to hear the packing case come down from off the top of the wardrobe, but there was silence, and silence like argument, worried her equally. She tried to enlist the rest of the family in her sense of urgency. But they told her that she was wrong to have brought the matter up again and that she should say no more about it, and it would all blow over. But she worried desperately over his possible departure. Every day, she went to his room to see if anything had changed, and she took his suitcase and hid it in her own wardrobe. At heart she knew she couldn't stop him, and it was this that worried her most of all.

A few weeks later, they were having supper together. The subject of Norman's move had not been mentioned for some time, and Mrs Zweck, although checking every day on the presence of his suitcase in her wardrobe, felt easier about the whole affair. After supper, Norman went to his room, which he did almost every evening, to study. The girls washed up and Mrs Zweck got on with her knitting. It was like any other evening when they all sat together in the flat, each intent on their own occupations. Except that tonight it was very silent. Mrs Zweck wondered what Norman was doing, but fearful of provoking a scene, she refrained from going to his room. Instead, she went to the wardrobe to check that the suitcase was there. She came back to the kitchen satisfied. It was getting late. Rabbi Zweck was still reading.

'Abie,' she said, 'is late. Go see what Norman is doing.'

'He's working. Leave him alone,' he said.

'Bella, go see what Norman is doing.'

'Leave him alone,' Rabbi Zweck said. 'A boy can't be on his own a while?'

She waited, restless. After a while, she got up. 'I'll go,' she said. Rabbi Zweck stayed her. 'Let him be, he's a big boy already. Let him be himself,' he said, as gently as he could. 'A little independence he needs. Then he won't be shouting always to leave home.'

She sat down again, and at the sound of Norman's door opening, she relaxed, and took up her knitting. She got through half a row, when her fingers seemed suddenly paralysed. Without looking up, she saw his shape in the doorway, and it was as if she suffered a black-out. It was his overcoat, filling the doorframe, that momentarily blinded her. She daren't look him in the face, so she lowered her eyes to his feet, and there beside him, was an old suitcase that she had never seen before. She looked at her son, put her hand to her heart, and brought out one of a stock of ready-made moans. Rabbi Zweck stared at Norman. He wished that if he were so bent on going, he would have gone when they were all out, when no one would attempt to stop him. 'You going out?' he said softly.

'I'm leaving,' Norman said. 'I'm not going away for ever,' he added, between his mother's moans. 'I'll come back and see you.' He too now wished he had gone without leave-taking, and he felt himself weaken before his mother's blackmail. There was nothing to stop him picking up his case and getting out, but he was rooted there, cursing her groaning. Then she spoke, after a deeply-drawn stuttered sigh. 'What for you wait?' she said.

'My blessings you waiting for?' She stood up and went towards him. Esther tried to stop her. 'Let him go,' she whispered.

'Another one,' Mrs Zweck turned on her. 'Are you also thinking of going? You see,' she yelled triumphantly at Norman, 'how the family is finished? You can do this to your mother and father? To send us both to an early grave?'

Rabbi Zweck looked at her helplessly. Logically, Norman's leaving was at the worst, upsetting. He knew it wasn't going to kill anybody. But he wasn't too sure of Sarah. Her whole life had been built around Norman, until Norman as a person had been swallowed whole. She would die a little if he left. Of that there was no question. He looked at Norman and saw the beginnings of surrender in him. He wanted to take his side, but he was afraid and for the first time in his married life, he did not like his wife. His own non-participation annoyed him; Bella too had opted out. Only Esther had made the slightest protest. There they sat, timid and neutral. Sarah had colonized them all.

'All right then,' he heard Norman say. 'I'll stay.'

He looked at his son and he was filled with an overwhelming pity, for the weakness that he had inherited from himself. He wanted to smile at him, but it might have been mistaken for a smile of triumph. So he looked at him and tried to convey that he had understood the damage that his wife had done. He heard Sarah give a scream of relief, and then, to give her relief expression, she raised her hand to strike him, partly to unburden herself, and partly to make sure that her son would never have such thoughts again. Rabbi Zweck jumped automatically to his feet and stayed her hand mid-air. He clenched his fist around the cuff of her sleeve, and placed her arm at her side.

Rabbi Zweck sat up on the bed. He saw his fist opening, and in a flash he knew the memory of the lace cuff on the dress. The recollection of the incident had saddened him. He wondered how responsible it was for Norman's present condition. But who knew when it began, or why it had happened at all.

He heard Bella coming upstairs from the shop, and he was glad that he was not alone.

15

That night, the first night in many years that he had lain in his marriage bed, Rabbi Zweck was taken ill. At first, he would not acknowledge it. The pain in the upper arm and around the heart, had become so familiar that he had accepted it as part of the ageing process that was inevitable. Moreover, he felt that if he ignored it, it would cease to exist. But this time he was frightened. Tentatively, he moved his legs to the empty side of his unfamiliarly large bed, and he felt very alone. He thought of calling for Bella, but he doubted whether he had enough strength to make himself heard. He lay quite still, as the pain intensified.

He knew he had to cry out, and he mouthed what he thought was Bella's name, but it was his straining call for 'Sarah' that Bella heard from her bedroom, and she rushed to her father's side. When she saw him struggling to hide the pain and his fear, she busied herself with calling the doctor, and making him as comfortable as she could, in order to postpone her own anxiety. She told him to lie quite still, and she sat by his side, guarding his immobility, until the doctor arrived. She watched anxiously as the doctor examined him, trying not to think about the consequences of her father's death. She found herself blaming Norman for it all, and the long heart-break that Esther had caused them. But it would be she, she knew, who all her life had given them trouble-free comfort, it would be she who would feel most guilty.

As the doctor unbuttoned her father's pyjamas, she felt suddenly embarrassed. She was able to look after him, and to mother him when he was fully clothed, but in his nakedness, he became a man, and her father, and she left the room in respect for his privacy. She waited outside a long time until the doctor came out. 'How is he?' she whispered.

'He's had a mild heart-attack,' Dr Jacobs said. 'He's sleeping now, and if he takes it easy, he'll recover. But he must take it very easy. He must stay in bed for at least a month. He must not get up at all. Another attack would be very dangerous. How old is your father, by the way?'

Bella had never associated years with her parents, and she could only make the wildest guess at her father's age. Your span of years didn't seem to matter until you were dying, when friends could assess whether you'd had a good run or not, and doctors could safely ascribe natural causes to a patient's condition.

'Can you manage to look after him?' Dr Jacobs said. 'It's going to be a full-time job. I could get him into hospital of course, but what with Norman being away, between visits you wouldn't have any time at all.'

'I'll get Auntie Sadie,' Bella said.

Dr Jacobs remembered Auntie Sadie from Mrs Zweck's last illness. Her efficiency and heartiness frightened him, but he nodded his approval. 'If Auntie Sadie is willing, one of the family is always better, of course.' Bella doubted that after the Norman experience, but she let it pass.

'How is Norman, by the way?' Dr Jacobs asked.

'He's getting better,' Bella said. It was a meaningless phrase. She was beginning to wonder what better was, as far as Norman was concerned.

'It's an extra worry for your father,' Dr Jacobs said. 'How soon d'you expect him home?'

'He has to stay for another three weeks,' Bella said, 'then it's up to the doctors. I don't know,' she said weakly.

'It's a bad business with Norman. And you've always been such a good daughter,' he said. He was being sorry for her, and only increased her own sense of self-pity. She wished he would go away. 'Will he really get better?' she asked, 'my father I mean.'

'If he doesn't exert himself, as I said, he'll get over this one. After that, in any case he must stop working in the shop, and he must generally take things easy. Here's a prescription. I've written down the instructions. I'll come again tomorrow morning.'

She saw him out. She was glad her father was sleeping. She needed time to learn how to face his illness in his presence. She wondered whether she should tell Norman, or write to Esther, but she knew that both were pointless and she swelled with the old anger that she had to bear the brunt alone. There was Auntie Sadie of course, but for all her goodness of heart, sickness had become a pleasure for her. Besides, Auntie Sadie had always been a source of disturbance for Bella, because she recognized how like each other they were. They were the family saints, suspected for their virtues, interminably used, and generally disliked for the guilts they evoked in other members of the family who were not playing their rightful parts. Still, it would be someone to face her father with, and there was much relief in that, for suddenly, in the face of his illness, which was so private and so physical a matter, she was shy of him. Yes, it was good that Auntie Sadie was coming.

Sadie was Rabbi Zweck's sister-in-law, Sarah's younger sister. She had never married. Her marriageable years had fallen squarely into the span of the Great War, during which time she had volunteered and trained as a nurse. There were many young men who sought her hand, but her nursing career took priority. Even when the war was over, she carried on with her work, hiring herself out as a private nurse. Her work so engrossed her that she did not notice her eligibility fall away, and it was not until other people finalized her state, with remarks like 'Pity you never married, Sadie,' that she realized that she had been left on the shelf.

But there was nothing spinsterish about Sadie. One look at her bank-book was evidence of a life led outside the nursing profession. Or rather, a life tangential to her nursing, for the borderline between professional and unprofessional care can be conveniently thin. There were numerous bequests, 'in token of her care and attention', from old widowers who had died on Sadie's hands, or more probably in her arms. There had come a time with each patient, when washing them and tucking them in had become faintly less business-like, and there was no doubt that, dying as they were, no one but Sadie could have given them a warmer send-off.

When Auntie Sadie arrived at Rabbi Zweck's, she put on her white coat. It gave her confidence, and it inspired, she hoped, more confidence in her patients. 'Well, who's been a naughty boy then,' she said, trundling into Rabbi Zweck's bedroom.

He was awake and more cheerful and he was glad to see her. She sat on the bed and held his hand, while he stroked hers, surprised at how happy he was that she had come. She was very different from Sarah, and so brought with her no disturbing reminders. She kissed him on his forehead.

'You must go see Norman,' he said.

'Abie,' she said firmly, 'it's for you I've come. To look after you. To make you better. After that, I stay a few days more, I'll go see Norman. All this worry with Norman,' she said, 'is no wonder you're not well. Norman needs you, Bella needs you, I also need you,' she added shyly. 'For us all you must get better.'

'You heard from Esther?' he whispered.

'Believe me,' Aunt Sadie said, 'she also needs you. But afraid I am to mention her name. She's well. Every letter she asks how are you. See her, Abie, for your own sake, I beg you, when you're better, let Esther come home.'

He sighed. 'I promised Sarah,' he said.

'Sarah, God rest her soul, will understand. But first, we get you better,' Sadie said.

Over the next few days, she talked to him little. She and Bella would sit at his bedside and sometimes read to him. And as the weeks passed, he gained strength and he became more and more difficult as a patient. He felt well enough to get up. He tentatively suggested that they should all visit Norman, because Norman played on his mind and he feared that his son would begin to miss him and worry about his health. But Sadie and Bella wouldn't allow him out of his room. They tried to get him to talk to Norman on the phone, but he looked upon that as a kind of abdication, and in any case, he thought it would arouse Norman's suspicions. If he could speak on the phone, and that would tax him enough, then why couldn't he go and see him and set his heart at rest. But they forbade him, though they both knew that his anxiety for Norman retarded his progress. They were playing with time, hoping either for Norman's discharge or for Rabbi Zweck's recuperation.

After a month, Dr Jacobs suggested a few hours a day on a chair on the balcony, and he could get up for meals. Bella returned full-time to the shop and most of the day, Rabbi Zweck was alone with Sadie. He wanted to talk to her all the time about Norman, and she allowed it, because it was in a way a substitute for a visit. He told her over and over again, the story of the pills and his hallucinations, of the journey to the hospital and the subsequent visits. He told her about Billy, and he asked her and himself again and again, why people should have to suffer so. He felt better when he'd spoken to her, because she offered no advice and she blamed nobody. She only had sympathy and a deep-rooted conviction, that Norman would get better. When Norman had exhausted him, they talked about their families, Sarah's childhood, Sadie's memories of her mother, and her father whom Rabbi Zweck had known and loved. And he too would talk about his life, starting in the present which was more painful, then easing himself gently back into the past. Gradually he gained his strength. His sole purpose of recovery was to visit Norman.

16

For the past few weeks, Minister had been behaving in a very strange way. He had become, as it were, unprofessional. He had taken to giving Norman a week's supply in advance, as opposed to the daily ration that had been his custom. Norman suggested that his conduct as Minister of Health was becoming unethical, but Minister answered that it was easier to balance his books on a weekly basis. He talked as if he'd gone into the big time. He hinted that he had a large number of clients, and that they were spread over all the villas in the hospital, about twenty-five in all, that his business was getting so large, it was almost ready for a take-over.

Norman had no idea where Minister kept his stocks, or from where they were imported, and it would have been highly un- ethical for him to inquire. Regularly, twice a week, Minister had a visitor from outside, but it was not always the same man. His cousins, Minister would call them, and Norman could only conclude that they were the carriers, and that for security's sake, they were varied. But then there was the problem of where he kept them in the hospital. Men were pretty free to wander where they liked from ward to ward, and down to the workshops or the canteen. He could have been stockpiling any- where. And Minister's new system of weekly rationing landed Norman with the problem of storage. He was not afraid that he would be tempted to consume them all at one go. His memories of whiteless days were acute enough to stay his hand. But he had to find a place to keep them. He put his problem to Minis- ter. 'Any ideas?' he asked. 'You must know of a good few places.' Minister winked at him. 'Sorry mate,' he said. 'Top secret. You forget I'm in the Cabinet. You're as good as asking for a leak.'

Norman could see that no help would come from that quarter. He looked around the ward, but every nook and cranny was exposed. His bed and its iron frame offered no hiding place. He considered his person, but in a place like this, the least private thing was one's own body. He considered sewing a tuck in the counterpane, provided he could get hold of a needle, but then all the counterpanes were identical and could easily, in the course of bedmaking, be switched from one bed to another. He wrapped his dressing-gown about him, and looking down, found his solution. The dressing-gown, although the property of the institution, was the only thing that belonged exclusively to him. He sat on the bed, and idly picked up the hem. It was broad enough, and its width all the way round was enough to contain at least a month's supply, without any undue weight or encumbrance. Casually he began to unpick at the stitching. After a few minutes he had made a decent enough break and he stuffed the three cellophane packets inside. He manoeuvred them down to the corner of the hem, and flattened them out. Then he stood up and watched how it hung. They were invisible. He walked over to Minister's bed. Minister's dressing-gown was draped over the counterpane. He fingered all around the hem, but it was empty, and he wondered again where Minister kept them.

It was still early in the morning and the patients were already out on the lawns. Norman went outside. It was a fine day, and there was a general air, as there was on some days in the hospital, of well-being. Often such a day ended in a storm, and usually inside the ward. That morning, when he'd first woken up, Norman thought he'd seen them again, but they were not yet clear enough – or in sufficient quantities to identify. Yet despite this, he too caught the feeling of well-being, armed as he was with a week's supply, and more when it was needed, and proud of his newfound hiding place. He joined Minister on the lawn.

Minister had no close friends in the ward. He didn't play chess and only rarely did he play ping-pong. He read little, and his pastime was to sit and stare. People were wary of joining him, and he was excluded from most of the groups. Because Minister regarded any gathering of three or more as a Cabinet meeting, he would rattle off the time-honoured minutes that he knew by heart of previous meetings that had never taken place, then he would ask for, and give back an agenda, address the meeting, ask questions, propose and receive a vote of thanks. All this regardless of anyone else's conversations. Once entangled in this procedure, it was difficult to withdraw, because although every man's madness, except one's own, was a monstrous repetitive bore, neverthless, it had to be respected. You didn't walk out on someone else's lunacy. You grinned and bore it, and firmly believed that they should be put away. And so Minister was usually alone, and it was at your peril that you joined him.

Nevertheless, Norman walked towards him. He was sitting in a deck-chair. He was still in pyjamas, and he'd managed to hold on to his own dressing-gown, a threadbare woollen affair, studded with cigarette holes. It was wrapped tightly around him. Norman looked directly at the hem, but noticed that it was narrow and unstitched practically the whole way round. He wore his boots as always – Minister shunned the ward slippers – his boots seemed to guarantee his identity as Minister of the Crown. They had a high shine and reached over his ankles, with black leather tabs jutting out at the back and catching in the hem of his pyjama trousers. Norman pulled up a chair beside him.

'You solved your problem, then?' Minister whispered. Minister only whispered when he wasn't being a Minister. In his role as health superintendent, he spoke loudly and with confidence. As a rank and filer, and Norman never discovered his real name, he whispered, sadly and timidly.

'Yes, I found somewhere,' Norman said.

Minister was not curious. He just stared ahead. Norman sensed that something was disturbing him. 'Something the matter?' he said.

'She's coming. She's coming this afternoon, but if she comes anywhere near my bed, I'll break 'er bloody back.' 'She' could only refer to his mother.

'It's only an hour or so,' Norman said. He couldn't think of any other consolation to offer, except that whatever it was that Minister dreaded, was terminable.

'She'd better not come near me,' Minister muttered again.

'What's so wrong with her?' Norman said. He was sorry he had asked. It was too personal a question for such a place. Though in the hospital the men's bodies were public, as public as their aberrations, it was not done to inquire into their cause. The scabs and scars were visible enough, what lay behind them, was the only privacy a man could hold on to. 'Doesn't matter,' he said. 'I don't really want to know.'

'They really ought to frisk visitors at this place,' Minister shouted. He was back in the Cabinet. 'There's no knowing what the bastards bring in on them. 'Ow am I supposed to keep this place clean, with all the scum coming and going, in and out, walking over my floors.' He spoke with the charwoman's possessive. 'There's no knowing what they bring in on them.'

Norman was weary of Minister's tirade. He wanted him to come out of the Cabinet. 'Is he coming?' he asked. 'The new husband, I mean.'

Minister retained his post. 'I tried to keep 'im out of the meeting,' he shouted, 'but the old cow voted 'im in. Democracy, she calls it. My arse. What this country needs is a dictatorship. If I 'ad my way, there'd be no one coming to soil this place. It 'ud be the only 'ealthy spot left in the world. Yes, 'e's coming,' he went on. 'They'll both walk into this place like they owned it. She'll be covered in cow-pads, and 'e'll 'ave a cock 'anging out of each eye.' He was trembling with anger and fear. Then without another word, he got up and walked back towards the ward. Norman looked after him and then followed. At the door of the ward, he waited. Minister was inside at the ward sink. Norman watched him, and he counted the glasses of water with which Minister was flushing himself. Fourteen in all. There seemed no quenching to his thirst at all, but only a desperate need to cleanse his soul of his mother's droppings. After the fourteenth glass, he moved away from the sink. He took a few steps, then he hesitated and returned. Four more glasses. Then, shrugging his shoulders with the painful futility of it all, he dragged his big boots off towards the bed.

Norman returned to the lawns. He went back to his chair, moving Minister's a little way off. There was an after-presence in Minister's chair and he wanted to be rid of it. He liked him well enough, but with that edge of hostility that was natural in a relationship of one entirely dependent on another. He didn't want to think about him, but it was difficult to put him out of his mind. The water-drinking episode had sickened him, and he wished he'd never seen it, and the thought of Minister's big boots dragging him away from his well, moved him un-utterably. There was a kind of inbuilt doom about Minister, and today, more than any other, Norman felt infected by it, and it seemed only enhanced by the bright sun that filtered through the trees on the lawn and the dreadful bonhomie of the patients joking amongst themselves about their own unenviable state. He shut his eyes, and the sun and their laughter pierced them. He turned his face into the canvas of the deck-chair. It was warm against his cheek, but it was dark and comforting. He wondered about his father. Over the past few weeks, he'd tried not to think about him. It was at least a month since he had seen him. Bella fobbed him off with excuses. The journey was too long for him; it was too much of a strain, or he was busy. She had flatly denied that he was ill, but he knew in his heart that she was lying. But what angered him most, was not so much his father's condition, but that it should be kept secret from him, as if he were suddenly an outsider in the family, a contemptible stranger who couldn't begin to understand. He wondered whether in fact, he had always been an outsider in the family, and whether he had so placed himself, or whether his parents and sisters had so elected him. He worried about his father. He felt sure that he was ill, that no inconvenience or strain had precluded his former visits. He wondered suddenly whether he would ever see his father again and a terrible anxiety shook him.

He got up quickly and went back into the ward. He saw that Minister was sleeping and he was glad for him, and wished himself likewise. He took some money out of his drawer and went down the corridor to the phone. He knew there could be no reply in the middle of the morning. They would both be downstairs in the shop. But he had to verify that nothing was wrong at home. Suddenly he felt an overwhelming respon-sibility for his whole family. He wanted to care for them all, even Esther, whom he could now name without bitterness. He wanted desperately to go home and he cursed the white that was keeping him.

He dialled the number and idly hung the receiver on his finger, waiting for confirmation of a no-reply. Then, to his horror, a woman's voice, white-coated, and half recognizable, answered the phone.

'Hullo,' Norman shouted. 'Who's that for God's sake?' He was insulted by the presence of a stranger in his home, and he panicked at the familiarity of the voice.

There was an obvious hesitation at the other end of the line, followed by an embarrassed giggle.

'It's your old Auntie Sadie,' the voice said.

Norman felt his heart leap in fear. Auntie Sadie, who came only in crisis, who moved from one death-bed to another, collecting rattles like butterflies. 'What are you doing there?' he screamed at her.

'Just visiting,' she said innocently, but she was as unconvincing as an undertaker on a social call.

'Is Pop ill?' Norman whispered. He had to know the truth.

'Ill, ill?' Auntie Sadie said, with the repetition and surprise of a bad liar. 'What should be the matter with your father?'

'Can I speak to him then?'

'In the shop he is with Bella,' Auntie Sadie said quickly, and with a little more confidence.

'What are you doing there then?' he asked again.

'I'm visiting, Norman,' she said with finality. 'D'you want I should come to see you?'

'How long have you been there?' Norman hesitated.

'Yesterday I came,' Auntie Sadie said.

'How long are you staying?'

'It depends,' she said.

'What does it depend on?' Norman practically shouted at her.

'Until I outstay my welcome,' she laughed. That could have meant anything.

He now had grounds for his fear, and he made up his mind to plan his escape from the hospital and go home and see for himself. 'Is Bella coming this afternoon?' he said casually.

'I don't think so. Terry is ill, and the shop is busy.'

'What about Pop?'

'A bit tired he is. Such a long journey it is for him. You'll be home soon, please God. Another few weeks, they say.' She was trying to get off the subject of visits.

'Will *you* come then,' he asked, bringing her right back.

Again, the undeniable hesitation, 'I'll stay and keep your father company. In the shop,' she added.

'He's ill, isn't he,' Norman said quietly.

'Who's ill? Who should be ill?'

'It doesn't matter,' Norman said.

He put the phone down. He was now determined to get out of the place. He wondered if his father was dying and he offered a quick and silent prayer that he would wait until he could get home. He walked back to the ward. He knew he couldn't leave until after lunch. He would be missed too soon, and brought back before he had time to get far enough. He would bide his time until the visitors were due to arrive. In the confusion of their comings and goings, he could slip out quietly. His only problem was clothes. His father and Bella had refused to bring his clothes to the hospital, and he hadn't worried about that until now. He toyed with the idea of taking Minister's while he was asleep, but they would be much too large for him. In any case, the idea repelled him. He might catch his ministerial despair. He sat on his bed. He knew it was an insurmountable problem. A man couldn't go through the streets in broad daylight, dressed in pyjamas, and hope to pass unnoticed. He would have to wait until it was dark. Then he would slip out of the corridor window, on his way supposedly to the lavatory. Then he would start walking or risk a lift, if he could by nightfall think up a feasible story to tell the driver. He felt pleased with his decision and the nagging anxiety for his father, and his desperate need to see him, blinded him to the risks that he would be taking. He tried to picture the flat with Auntie Sadie upstairs, and Bella and his father in the shop. And Auntie Sadie looked wrong there all alone, and he couldn't see his father in the shop either. He didn't know how he could hold out till nightfall.

He gripped the sides of the bed, and stared at the floor. There they were again. Just a few of them, but enough to confirm their presence. It was only a matter of time before they multiplied. But what could you expect in a place as filthy as this one. He'd be glad to be home. In face of his other anxieties, he had forgotten the filth he had left in his own bedroom. For a moment he couldn't understand what he was doing in the place, and what kind of sickness was he supposed to have that he should land up with a bunch of lunatics. He sniffed to test whether they had brought their smell with them. But as yet, the air was clear and his body was free from irritation. He looked up from the floor and stared ahead of him. The sun pounded through the windows, and like a projector, threw dust-laden beams across the ward. 'Why can't they keep this bloody place clean?' he sobbed. He was terrified that they would come in their droves and crawl upon him before he could get out of the place and see his father. He couldn't cope with everything at the same time. He dared not think of the clothes problem, but he prayed for the dark to come quickly. 'Dear God,' he whispered, 'let him live, and I'll come off the pills, I promise.'

The nurse appeared at the door of the ward. 'Norman,' he shouted. 'You're wanted on the telephone.'

He stood up, but fear held him to his bed. 'He's dead,' he whispered to himself. He looked around the ward. It was practically empty. Minister slept in a sad heap on his bed. The sight of his sleeping figure filled Norman with fury. Why should anybody be unaware of his own agony. 'Minister,' he screamed across the ward.

Minister jumped up with a start, and fearing that his visitors had already arrived, he leapt out of bed and made for the door. Norman noticed that he still had his boots on.

'Norman,' the nurse called again. 'You're wanted on the phone.'

'Who is it,' he whispered.

'I think it's your father.'

He felt hot tears run down his face with a surge of relief and gratitude. He hurried to the phone.

When Auntie Sadie had finished speaking to Norman, Rabbi Zweck had called weakly from his bedroom, 'Who was it?' He

166

strained his voice to be heard. Auntie Sadie hurried to his room.
'It was the wrong number,' she said cheerfully.

'Such a long time with a wrong number,' he muttered.

She didn't deny it, but she was afraid to tell him the truth of the call for fear of upsetting him. For a moment, she hated Norman for what he was doing to his father. She made a show of tidying up the bed, and Rabbi Zweck gripped her hand as she plumped the pillows. 'Is Norman, isn't it?' he said.

She nodded her head.

'He's worried I don't go see him. He knows. I must talk to him,' he said decisively. 'Bring me please the phone.'

But Auntie Sadie was firm. He was in no state to talk to Norman. 'No,' she said. 'Is too much for you. You don't need extra worries. Wait, a few weeks you'll be up and about. You can go see him, or perhaps, please God, he'll come home.'

'Sadie,' he begged, 'is not enough worries the boy has got, he must worry also for his father. Bring please the phone. I should just talk to him.'

But Auntie Sadie went on tidying the already neat dressing-table.

'Sadie,' Rabbi Zweck said. 'You already dusted. If I know he worries my son, then I also worry. Is no good for me I should worry. I feel better I should speak to him. Bring please the phone.'

'All right,' she capitulated, 'but only for a few minutes.'

'Just so long he knows I'm alive,' Rabbi Zweck said. He smiled at her as she left the room.

Aunt Sadie pulled the telephone across the hall. Fully stretched, it just managed to reach the door of the bedroom. She helped him out of his bed, sat him in a chair and wrapped a blanket around him. She dialled the number and gave him the receiver, while with her handkerchief, she wiped the sweat from his forehead.

'Please, is the hospital?' Rabbi Zweck asked. 'I should speak to Norman Zweck.' He gave the name a defiant dignity, and he engaged a smile on his face in preparation for the cheer he would put into his voice. While he waited, he pressed the receiver close to his ear, anxious to be part of any of the sounds of Norman's habitation. He heard fading footsteps, and a clatter of cutlery. Then there was a long silence, broken by a distant scream of someone's name. The echo of the name down the phone unnerved him, not only because of the pitch, but because there was something in the voice that was vaguely familiar. He heard a scuffling of boots, and silence again. The sweat dripped from his forehead and he shivered.

'Is not good for you,' Auntie Sadie said helplessly.

'Wait, wait,' he said. 'He is sleeping perhaps.'

'Then let him sleep.' Auntie Sadie could not hide the malice in her voice. 'You should be sleeping too.'

'Is a long time,' Rabbi Zweck murmured.

'Let me hold it for you.'

But he wouldn't give her the receiver. He wanted to hear Norman from the ward to the telephone and all the sounds that attended him.

When Norman reached the phone, he lifted the receiver to his ear, and listened to his father's breathing. 'Pop?' he said softly.

'Norman. Norman. What's this I should be ill? Who says? Auntie Sadie runs down to the shop. Tells me such a story. I'm ill all of a sudden.' He laughed. He was pleased with his tale. He nodded at Auntie Sadie and she returned her approval.

'You haven't been to see me for almost a month,' Norman said. 'What's the matter with you?'

Rabbi Zweck hesitated. 'In the shop,' he said brightly, 'suddenly we're so busy. And Bella comes to see you. When you come home I see you.'

'What's that bitch doing there?'

Rabbi Zweck pressed the receiver hard against his ear, but Auntie Sadie had caught the word. She shrugged her shoulders. 'Holiday,' she mouthed at Rabbi Zweck.

'A holiday,' he practically shouted into the phone. 'Imagine,' he said, 'your Auntie Sadie takes a holiday.' He giggled.

'Where is she now?' Norman said.

'Downstairs. In the shop. I ran to phone you. She's with Bella.'

'Why can't you come and see me?' he asked again.

Rabbi Zweck sighed. 'To tell the truth,' he said, and it was a half-truth he was telling him. 'I get upset. With the long journey, and the place you know I don't like.'

'You think I enjoy it?' Norman said. 'It's bloody filthy here. You'd think they'd clean the floors once in a while. The whole bloody place is crawling.'

Auntie Sadie saw a pallor spread over Rabbi Zweck's cheek. 'Good-bye, good-bye,' she mouthed anxiously.

Rabbi Zweck felt helpless. He couldn't understand how all the symptoms of Norman's illness seemed suddenly to have returned. He didn't know what to say so he giggled again nervously. But he was sick at heart, and his eyes were burning.

'It's nothing to laugh at,' Norman said angrily. His anxiety for his father had already waned, and he was able to concentrate on his age-old problem. 'Everybody's complaining,' he went on. 'One of the patients is on strike. He won't go to bed because the sheets are dirty. He sits in a chair all night. Maybe I'll join him.' Norman was not confident as yet in his own argument to hold it alone, and he had to invent support for it. 'The whole fucking ward'll be on strike if they don't do something about it.'

Rabbi Zweck winced. He wanted to put the phone down and weep. For a moment he felt indignant at the dirty surroundings his son was subjected to, and he resolved to write a strong letter to the management. He was ready to believe Norman rather than acknowledge his son's sickness. But he knew that dirty sheets were no more present than silver-fish. He couldn't encourage his son's madness. 'It'll get better,' he said weakly. 'You'll see, in a few days, is better. In a few days, I come to see you. Go back to bed now. Is sleep you need.'

'Jesus,' Norman screamed, 'you keep on about sleep. Why don't you bloody well put me to sleep and have done with it once and for all.'

'Norman, Norman,' Rabbi Zweck pleaded.

'Pop,' Norman said quietly, 'you've got to get me out of here.'

'I come. I come. In a few days I come,' Rabbi Zweck said. 'I'll see. I'll talk to the doctor. Auntie Sadie's calling me,' he said with sudden inspiration. He couldn't take much more of it. 'I must go. In a few days. I come to see you.'

'If you want,' Norman said helplessly. 'Tell Bella to bring my clothes when she comes,' he said. He was confirmed in his blunted imagination that there was nothing wrong at home, and he had given up all ideas of escape. But a suit of clothes was always handy.

'I'll tell her,' Rabbi Zweck said. 'She'll come tomorrow. Look after yourself,' he added. 'I see you soon.'

'Good-bye, Pop,' Norman said. 'Take it easy.'

Rabbi Zweck put down the phone and sank back into the chair.

'I told you you shouldn't talk. Look how it upsets you.'

'Is the same, he is,' he moaned. 'Exactly the same. What they do in such places?' he added bitterly. 'At least,' he added, 'about me, he's not worried any more. That's something.'

'You must go to sleep,' Auntie Sadie said. 'You must rest. Only rest will make you better. Come. I'll take away the pillows.' She helped him back into bed. Rabbi Zweck took hold of her hand. 'Sadie,' he said, 'very hard I've been thinking. And I know I promised Sarah, God rest her soul. But not for ever I shall live. I know it. Poor Sarah, she didn't know. She was getting better, she thought. Remember how we planned a holiday? Poor Sarah. But I, I know. How long should I live, Sadie? This attack, another attack, who knows?'

'Don't talk like that,' Sadie said.

'Listen to me Sadie,' he gripped her hand very hard. 'I've been thinking.' He paused, loosening his grip, and letting his hand drop on the eiderdown, he said, 'I should like to see my Esther.'

Auntie Sadie was glad of his request, but sad that he had to be so ill before he gave up his pride. 'I'll write to her,' she said. 'You sleep now while I write to her a letter. She'll come soon. Something for you to look forward to,' she smiled, tucking him under the chin.

'So good you are to me Sadie,' he said. 'Now, I'll sleep.'

She closed the door quietly. She would write immediately and she prayed that Esther would get to her father on time.

When Norman got back to the ward, they were laying the table for lunch. He didn't feel hungry; the white always took away his appetite. Yet he had to make a show of eating or the nurses would get suspicious. Sometimes he and Minister managed to dish their food on to the plates of the other patients who, although they had been robbed of all else, still retained their crude and gruff appetites. Minister was still sleeping. A nurse called over to him, and Norman went up to his bed. He would wake him gently, knowing the fears that would accompany his waking. 'Minister,' he whispered, 'it's lunch-time.' He wanted to make it clear he wasn't waking him for any other purpose. Minister turned over. He was already awake and full of dread of the coming visit. Wearily he got out of bed. 'Why don't you take off your boots?' Norman said.

'I may be called suddenly to a meeting,' he said. 'In any case, they're a damn sight cleaner than the beds in this place.' Norman heartily agreed with him and helped him on with his dressing-gown. The feeling of kinship between them was mutual. Minister suddenly put his arm round Norman's shoulder and sat him down on the bed next to him. 'Listen,' he whispered. 'I wouldn't admit this to anyone else, but I think both of us might be lunatics. I mean, everyone says the place is clean, and you and me can see with our own eyes it's bloody filthy, so is there something wrong with them or is it us.'

'Let's have our lunch,' Norman said. He himself had often been plagued with similar doubts, but he dared not give in to them, and he didn't want Minister confusing him further.

Minister didn't move. 'I wish I was dead,' he whispered. 'I've 'ad enough of it all. Enough of the lousy Cabinet too. A lot of jerks. Nobody listens to me no more. They think *you're* nuts as well. What's the use.' He tied his dressing-gown around him. 'The only thing I got left is kicking the old bucket,' he said, 'and even that'll belong to my lousy Mum when it's all over. There must be somewhere in this godforsaken 'ole where you can go and do it and keep it for yourself. Just fancy, you and me,' he said, 'living a whole bloody life-time in this filth.'

'Let's go and have lunch,' Norman said. He sympathized with Minister, but he wasn't altogether happy with the way Minister equated his problem with his own. He'd never had any doubts at all that Minister was off his nut, and only very occasionally had he had vague doubts about his own sanity. But today, on the threshold of his ravings, he had no doubts at all. He felt pity for all the madmen who surrounded him, nurses and doctors included. He took Minister's arm and led him to the table. They had always managed to reserve a table for themselves. They were each so much alone, that they were landed together, and the other patients donated them such privacy as they could. Today, however, their table was already occupied by a new patient who obviously didn't know the form. He sat there, timidly staring in astonished disbelief at the horrible mixture of food on the plate in front of him. He looked up and saw Norman and Minister standing on either side of him. It felt like an arrest, and automatically he got up, and Norman sensed at least part of the man's history. He knew just how he had been brought to this place, and probably not for the first time, because his reaction had the immediacy and automation of long-standing habit. 'Doesn't matter,' he said, 'sit down. There's room for all of us.'

But Minister refused to join them. ' 'E's new,' he said suspiciously, ' 'ow d'you know where 'e's been, and what 'e's brought in on 'im, on 'is person, I mean. You can't be too careful in a place like this. 'E should be vaccinated,' he shouted, 'God knows where 'e's been till now. And we can catch it. Keep away mate,' he said addressing himself to Norman, 'every man for 'isself in this place.' He moved over to another table, and sat down where the filth was known and less fearful. The three men already at the table ignored his arrival, and Minister sat down in isolated splendour. ' 'Oo wants this muck?' he shouted. The three men shoved their plates forward without looking at him. He doled it out in three parts, very meticulously, first the meat, then the potatoes and vegetables, and with less success, the gravy. 'God knows where that lot's been,' he muttered. 'That one what's sitting over there. Why didn't no one wake me up when 'e came? No one notifies me and you all bloody well know it's my job,' he shouted at them.

'You having any visitors this afternoon, Minister?' one of his table-mates said. He wanted to get back to some normal conversation, but he couldn't have chosen a more tactless topic. Minister got up silently and left the table. He walked down to the cleaning cupboard at the end of the ward and he took out a disinfectant spray. Then he walked to Norman's table, and standing a few feet from the object, according to the instructions of the label, he sprayed the newcomer with the liquid. He stayed to empty the whole bottle, while his object, conditioned to a life-time of subjugation, sat, unmoving. Minister planted the empty bottle on the table and went back to his bed. The newcomer looked at his disinfected dinner and pushed it away. 'You can have mine if you like,' Norman said. 'I'm not hungry.'

The man shook his head and Norman left him. He had no curiosity about the newcomer and was completely indifferent to his silent despair. He decided to go out again on the lawn. At least that would be clean. They wouldn't be there, crawling all over the place, and if they were, better outside where they belonged, than in the ward where they were driving him as mad as the rest of them.

The sun was now settled directly over the grass, and he curled himself into the warm canvas of his chair. He would sit out the visiting hours; he didn't want to witness Minister's afternoon. But the sun began to irritate him and he dragged his chair underneath a tree. He was glad that most of the men were still inside. He could not bear their outdoor laughter, yet, at the same time, the general silence of the place was frightening. It had been the same kind of day, with the same kind of warm threatening stillness that had witnessed Billy's breakdown; it was the tedium of constant light and heat that had screwed his brain to cracking point. Norman felt that if he stayed out in the light much longer, he himself would crumble. But the alternative was the ward, in his bed, crouched under the darkness of the blankets, but therein lay an even greater menace. He was in the position of not knowing what to do with his body, neither did he know which part of him was begging a hiding-place. He had to hide his eyes away, because it was they that saw them, and his nose that smelled them, and his body itself that itched with them, these too needed concealment. But his mind was clear and unafraid. Yet his body and his mind were indivisible, and he would have to carry them both under the blankets, assuring his mind that he understood its immunity. The sun filtered through even under the thickly branched tree, and it frightened him, because he knew it was going to cause trouble. The only dark room in the hospital was the lavatory, but you could never lock yourself in. You had to announce your going, and your stay there was timed. It was this horrifying lack of privacy that he knew would finally destroy him.

He got up, kicked over the chair and idled back down the corridor. He counted the tables alongside. Five of them and the fourth sported a tea-stained cloth that had not been changed since his arrival. He already had a terrible familiarity with the place, a kind of intimacy one has with one's own home, to the extent of overlooking certain inadequacies because they have become liveable with. He rarely thought of his own home now. Its geography had become blurred. When he did occasionally think about it, he saw no lay-out of rooms. He picked up single images, Bella in her white socks, David's favourite chair, his mother plaiting the Sabbath loaves, and Esther poring over her books. Together, they seemed to him the driving force that had propelled him into his present isolation.

He turned down the covers of his bed, and carefully wiped the sheets with sweeping movements of his hand. As he got into bed, he noticed Minister staring at him from the other side. He was reminded of his first day's admission to the place and that stare that had so unnerved his father. He pushed himself down between the sheets, and covered his head. It was dark and warm inside, and he tried to concentrate on just these two comforts. Then as he grew used to it, it was no longer dark, and the heat was stifling. Perhaps he could smother himself, he thought, but he didn't want to die. He just wanted to sleep it all away and to wake up when everything was clean and touchable. He felt himself sweating and he ascribed that to the heat. Then his body itched and he put that down to the heat too. He had to. He had to lie to himself sometimes otherwise he would have had to surrender completely. He scratched his body and tried to think of other things to take his mind off his pain. He wondered whether Minister was still staring at him, and he peeped above the blankets across to his bed. But Minister wasn't there. He was probably in the lavatory preparing for his ordeal.

They were clearing away the lunch plates and the newcomer still sat at his table. It would be at least an hour before the visitors began to arrive, and that was the worst time of all, the waiting, and the terrible fear that you couldn't entertain them while they stayed. The muttered rehearsed soliloquies in the garden. 'How are things at home then?' 'How's the car?' 'Yes, I'm much better, thank you,' and the long painful silences that no amount of rehearsal could overcome. 'Yes, you'd better go now or you'll miss the bus. See you next week,' and the mono- logues would come to an end and start up all over again, with no variation from week to week, peppering the smooth lawns with droppings of vocabulary, and relieved at last to be called to face their ordeal.

Norman watched the newcomer make a move to rise from the table. Then he thought better of it, and sat down again. A beam of sunlight shot suddenly through the ward, and Norman hid from it, cursing. He lay under the blankets and enjoyed the dark again, but the heat welled up on him. He heard the tea-bell which rang only a quarter of an hour before visiting-time, and he marvelled that he'd been able to lie in his own sweat for so long. He decided to get permission for a bath. He would sponge himself cool with cold water, and already at the thought of it, he felt much better.

He got out of bed and went to the nurse's room. The nurse told him that Minister was bathing but that he should be out soon, because he was expecting visitors. 'Sprucing himself up for his Mum,' the nurse smiled. 'You got anyone coming today?'

'No,' said Norman with relief. 'But I'd sooner be out of the ward when the visitors come. It depresses me. A bath's a pretty good way of killing time.'

'It's open,' the nurse said. 'Tell Minister to hurry, and you can have fifteen minutes yourself. I'll be up then.' He handed Norman a clean towel from the cupboard behind him. As he passed it over, his eyes narrowed, and still smiling, he said, 'You're always bathing, aren't you?'

Norman laughed. 'It's this place,' he said, 'it's dirtier than a bloody coal-mine.'

'Well,' the nurse said generously, 'you're entitled to your own opinion, I suppose.'

Norman walked down the corridor. The sun pierced the glass

windows that lined one side, and again Norman was assailed by the foreboding that had dogged him all day. But at least, upstairs in the bathroom, there was a dark rubber curtain he could draw and keep it for a while out of his sight.

He reached the top of the stairs and saw it again, dribbling through the bathroom door, and he was surprised that Minister, who hated the light as much as he, hadn't bothered to draw the curtain. He would call him and wait outside. He valued his own privacy sufficiently to have respect for someone else's. 'Minister,' he called softly. There was no answer. Norman thought Minister couldn't have heard him. A man often became deaf in his bath. So he called again, louder this time. Again there was no answer, but what disturbed Norman, was not so much Minister's silence, but the absolute and overall silence that practically shrieked from behind the door. He wanted to open it, but he was frightened. He dared not analyse his fear but he knew it was bound up with the shaft of sunlight beneath the door, and the terrible silence within.

Gently he pushed the door slightly ajar with his foot, and he looked through the narrow crack. He saw the top end of the bath. He noticed how dirty the taps were, and he got over with cursing them and the establishment before he took in the rest of what was visible. Minister's one foot was resting between the hot and cold taps. The other had fallen into the water. There was nothing very strange in this position, except that both feet were clad in Minister's boots, and a number of little cellophane packets were floating around his ankle, like gathering scum. Even this strange sight did not unduly worry Norman as he stood there in the crack of the door. It was explainable. Minister never took his boots off, and he'd probably fallen asleep in the bath. Yet Norman felt suddenly very cold. There was something else about the scene that he refused to acknowledge, and nothing would have induced him to have opened the door wider and investigate. He thought that the water in the bath was red, a very deep red at times, and sometimes streaky. He thought of his family's favourite word, and in these circumstances he was more than prepared to accept it. He was hallucinating. He was 'seeing' things. They were wrong about the silver-fish, of course, utterly wrong, but all men saw things in times of stress, and today was one of those times for him, with that terrible sun and the men's silences. So he stared at the water for a long time, and willed it to be an illusion. But as he grew colder, the water seemed to deepen in colour. He shivered. He had to acknowledge it. The red water was no more hallucination than the silver-fish, and he was betraying himself even to doubt it. If he, Norman Zweck, saw something, then it was positively there. And this blood water was no exception. Looking through the crack in the door, and feeling the cold crawl over him, he thought of David, and he sickened at the recollection. Most people could live a whole lifetime, without once witnessing its termination, wilful or otherwise. Why in God's name, he sobbed to himself, had he been so elected, cast as some ugly ubiquitous coroner. He pushed the door open wide.

Minister lay with his head submerged. His arms had turned blue to the elbows, and they floated lifelessly. The boot of the foot in the water, had rotted with the heat. The sole had come apart from the uppers, revealing Minister's hiding-place. Norman was tempted to gather the packets of white together, but he was reminded of his last case at the Bar, when Bertie Cass had taken his mother's ring from off her dead finger. He watched them floating there, and he resisted, but the waste appalled him.

He rushed out of the door. He felt tears running down his face. Sometimes he had pitied Minister, sometimes he had had compassion for him, but never, until this moment had he truly loved him. He was shivering with cold and crying uncontrollably. He was crippled with his panic, yet for the first time in many long weeks, he wanted so much to live. He ran down the corridor screaming, 'He's dead, he's dead.'

At one of the tables, a couple were sitting, and Norman could only suppose that the woman was Minister's mother. He took her by the shoulders and shook her like a medicine bottle. 'You killed him,' he screamed, 'you fucking whore. You killed him.'

The nurse took him to his annexe, and when he could speak, he brought up his story. The nurse made a telephone call, and within a matter of minutes, the affair was under cold and clinical control. All visitors and the patients who expected them, were sent out on to the lawns. Minister's visitors were taken care of by the doctor, and the general ward was locked. Only a few men remained inside, together with the newcomer, and they were asleep.

Norman sat on his bed, his face buried in his hands. The sun was beginning to trouble him again, and his grief was giving way to increased panic. He now realized that his source had been forever cut off. He now had but one week's supply, and the whiteless pain-racked days would be upon him. He fingered the edge of his dressing-gown and worked the little packets to the hole in the end. After a few minutes manoeuvring, he held his whole survival in his hands. He put one packet back in its hiding place in a split second of sanity to save against a rainier day. 'What the hell,' he muttered to himself, and emptying the pills on to his palm, he swallowed them whole.

He sat on his bed for about an hour, shielding his eyes from the sun, and peering at the sleeping figures around him. He could not think of Minister. When he tried, it was as if it had all happened many years ago, and he only had the vaguest recollection of the story, as if he had half-woken from a bad dream. What occupied him was the army of silver-fish on the floor. They were coming out of the blinding sun towards him, slowly in platoons, and with audacious confidence. He watched them come towards him, and at his feet, they gathered their forces for the superhuman climb up his body. He watched them, terror-struck, and heard their slow and regular breathing. As they moved, they left their droppings behind, and the whole length of the ward floor was carpeted with their tracks. He watched with horrible fascination how they manoeuvred themselves into little groups at his feet. He thought of lifting his foot, but he knew that if he tried to crush them, they would overwhelm him. There surely could be no greater terror in anybody's life, and although he loathed them, yet he had to acknowledge that they were sacred, that they were the only evidence of his own sanity. And so he watched them assemble like pilgrims at his feet. They had chosen him too, like his parents and his sisters, and he stood there, their reluctant disciple, rooted in fear. And suddenly they invaded him, and he was lost.

He opened his mouth to scream, but he heard nothing. At the end of the ward, he saw the Hoover, that had been hurriedly left, its cable dragging, when the news of Minister had come through. He ran down the ward, switched off the plug, and picked up the cable. Then, with a strength that astonished him, he ripped the cord in two. He spread out the coloured wires before switching it on again. Then he crawled along the floor to his bed, electrocuting them along the skirting. All this time, the newcomer had been watching him, and he let out a scream that woke the rest of the men and all were infected by Norman's panic. When he reached his bed, he stood up and attempted to apply the naked wires to his body. Two nurses rushed in and held him. He dropped the wire, and looked at them pleadingly. 'Put me to sleep,' he whimpered.

The nurse obliged, and whether it was the blinding sun or the needle that paralysed him, he never knew. His muscles turned to water, and he felt himself departing, and in his raging mind, he thanked them.

Over the next week there was an epidemic of breakdowns in the hospital, and a subsequent rash of deep sleeps. For when the Minister died, a business empire crumbled, and its clients were legion and broken.

17

Esther arrived the following day. Rabbi Zweck was sitting on the balcony when he heard the door bell ring. He was restless with anticipation, and he got up from his chair to give his body something to do. But standing up, he felt suddenly vulnerable, and he knew that if he had to go and meet her in the hall, he would collapse. It wasn't the physical exertion of standing on his feet, it was the feeling of being completely unprotected, and for this meeting, which he feared as much as he longed for, he needed support. So he sat down again in his chair. The arms encased him and he felt less exposed. It was much more a position of receiving, and that was what he was about to do with the daughter he had refused for almost twenty years.

He knew he had done wrong in rejecting her and it was not enough to excuse it with his loyalty to Sarah. He no longer felt sinned against and he hoped she would be able to forgive him. He would have to ask her about her husband, though he knew it would be painful, but that too, was part of her coming home.

He strained his ears to hear her voice, but Auntie Sadie and Bella were drowning it in their welcome. He hoped that they would leave them alone together, especially in the beginning when he would first see her. He would be guilty, embarrassed and excited in turn, and he didn't want witnesses. He turned his chair to face the door.

He watched the door open and he could hardly contain his excitement. The door-frame was empty for a while, and he could hear her hesitation outside. 'Esther,' he called. He thrilled at the name, and the flood of her childhood overwhelmed him. Her fair curls that he ruffled, and her wiry almost boyish frame, that he watched every morning running down the street to the school. It was this moving and vital image that he had carried in his mind daily through her long absence. So when she appeared in the doorway, he started a little, trying to hide his shock. He smiled at her but he suffered a terrible inner anger that he had so stubbornly missed out on her womanhood. Now her growth was past, her face and her figure was settled. She had grown fat and her face was lined. All that could happen to her now, was that the ageing of her body would intensify, but there could be no further radical change. He felt as if he'd walked out on the middle act of a play, and was trying to pick up the threads of the story.

But there was something more than the look of age that disturbed him. There was something radically wrong with her hair. Having accepted that she had to age, even though he wasn't there to sanction or to watch it, he would have expected her hair to have grown less fair, and perhaps to have thinned a little. But her hair was thick, very thick, and a dark brown, with no vestige of her early curls. In fact, it didn't look like hair at all. It looked coarse and hard, as if it had been cut out of a door-mat. And then the full meaning of what she had done, brought a lump to his throat and gave a bitter footnote to the twenty years that he had lost her. She had shaved her head for her marriage, and she was wearing the ritual wig, and Rabbi Zweck realized, that the marriage, which he had never allowed himself to accept, had been for her as meaningful as if she had married one of her own kind.

She saw his shock, but she had expected it, and so was better prepared. She was prepared too for what change she might see in him. He looked much older, but her own vanity did not allow her to be surprised. In her terms, fathers and mothers were always old people. But his obvious shock at her appearance angered her. What did he expect after all? Had he expected her to stunt her growth, to freeze-frame until he was ready to accept her again? 'I'm older,' she said from the door, 'and I'm happy.'

Her protest was too early and there was an edge of malice in her voice. But Rabbi Zweck took it as part of his punishment. 'So happy I am to see you,' he said simply. 'Come, let me look at you.'

She went towards him and they looked at each other for a long while. He could not accustom himself to the mat on her head, and he tried to avoid looking at it. Why, even Sarah, God rest her soul, and she was pious enough, why, even she hadn't gone that far when they were married. He thought perhaps that he should mention it, so that it would be open between them and less embarrassing.

'A *scheitel* I see you're wearing,' he ventured.

'I'm married, Poppa,' she said.

'Yes, yes. How is ... er ... John?' It was such a non-Jewish name to give utterance to, but he forced it out.

'He's well,' she said. 'He hopes you get better soon.'

She touched him on his sleeve and he realized they had not yet embraced each other. But that touch of hers had a finality about it. It was no prelude to a kiss; it was a gesture on its own terms, and he wondered whether she would give him much more. Perhaps he ought to make the first move. He wished that she were not so distant with him. His heart was bursting with his long-hoarded love, yet he was looking at a complete stranger. Surely there must be some magic word, some gesture that would return her to him.

'Norman's not well,' he said. He didn't know why he said it. Perhaps it was to enclose her once more in the family. 'Such a pity you never saw Momma,' he whispered. He was tying her gently into their past and present sorrow, he was welding her into his own tears, he was bringing her fully home. He heard her crying. She knelt by his side, and he took her into his frail arms, forcing himself to stroke her false protecting hair. 'You still have me,' he said, 'your old Poppa. Together we are,' he said, 'so now we stay together,' and he began to sob with her until she was no longer a stranger.

Now it was easier, and Bella and Auntie Sadie joined them. Esther did not speak about her life with John, and she was not offended that they could not refer to it. It was Rabbi Zweck who launched each topic of conversation. Events that had taken place since Esther's departure, either in her life or in theirs, were not spoken of, and so their conversation centred around their common memories. When they had recalled her old schooldays, the *cheder*, Rabbi Zweck's years as a minister, and remembered the odd highlights of those years, it seemed that nothing more was needed to reinstate her into the family. Then their conversation flagged with the avoidance of the subject of Norman. None of them was embarrassed by the silences. Families do not sit down to make conversation. They gather around for conference, the discussion of something quite specific, and when the silence between them became noticeable, Esther said, 'Tell me about Norman.'

Rabbi Zweck and Bella looked at each other. Both needed to tell the tale, but both knew that the telling was more painful than the keeping, and each wanted to save the other from that pain. So they both started together, and as it unwound itself, they shared it between them. It came out as less the story of Norman's condition, than of their own heart-ache, and this too, chained Esther to her return. She felt guilty that she had had no part of it. She was sorry for Norman, but it was their suffering that moved her, and she pictured them both, sitting around the same table, with her mother and Norman, after she had left the home. She had often seen them sitting there, and in her mind, she had known their agony. But it was only now that her own heart ached for what she had done.

She cursed Norman for what he had encouraged her to do, while all the family thought that he was innocent. She had often imagined how he had read out the letter to them, the letter that he himself had dictated. She imagined his feigned astonishment, his feigned accusation, his feigned misery. She wondered how he had come to terms with David's death, and whether he had yet admitted to himself that he was partly responsible. She thought of John and already missed him. She didn't love him any more. In fact, the loving had ceased many years ago. But the marriage had lasted for the simple reason that it had had to last. To have broken it would have made David's death even more meaningless. But she was entirely dependent on him as if her guilt were too heavy to be borne alone. Together over the years, they had shared the sad damage of what they had done, and alone, she was burdened and unsure. But if her father would forgive her, she would be ready to leave John, as she had been ready for many years, at the slightest hint of a reconciliation with her parents. And John, though he loved her deeply, would let her go for her own peace. But her mother had died without breathing her name, and she would have to settle for half their forgiveness. Her mother had never known the true story. Neither had her father. It was not as they thought. It wasn't a straightforward elopement, a marrying-out. In fact, when she'd left home, she'd not even been married. No, it was not as blunt as that, nor had it happened so quickly. It had started years before they had ever known.

She was in her last year at school, and she often went to the library to browse away among the books and sometimes to study. She knew John as a family friend. He had procured a special concession to borrow books from the reference library for her father, so he came often to the flat, armed with her father's requests. Though he was only a little older than Norman, those two had little to say to each other. It was her father that John came to see, because he loved listening to him, and over the years he had acquired a more than superficial knowledge of Jewish lore.

One day, Esther went to the library after school, and because it was raining, she stayed to read. His desk was in the middle of the floor, and he presided at it, flanked with files and telephones. She sat on the bench directly in front of his desk, not with any design, but because, unlike the others, it was empty. She read with little interest in the book, waiting for the rain to stop. From time to time, she would look up from the book and gaze out of the window, and once, she looked at him at his desk, and she thought he was staring at her. She went back to the book and pretended to read, but soon she looked up again, and he was staring at her still. She carried his look back with her to the book and she found herself trembling. His face was planted on the printed word, like the light of a lamp, that once seen, is carried elsewhere by the eye. She noticed for the first time, his thick black hair, high forehead, the eyes, gentle as a woman's. She was afraid to look up again. She stiffened her legs to keep her body still. She had an instinctive warning to get up and leave the library before looking up at him again. She got up, fearing that her trembling was noticeable, and as she made for the door, he called her. She hesitated, knowing that it was courting danger to go back, but she excused herself on the grounds that it would have been impolite to ignore him. As she walked over to his desk, her legs seemed to stiffen with an intense and giddy growing-pain. She no longer saw him in the context of her family. Such an association had, in that moment become impossible. As she neared his desk, he wondered whether he could ever visit her father again.

'My flat is only across the road,' he said. 'Go and shelter there. You'll get soaked if you go straight home. I'll be back in about half-an-hour.' He needn't have made any excuses. She took the key and the card on which he'd scribbled the address, as if she were expecting it, as if it were an arrangement of long-standing, and she went to his room to wait for him.

That was the beginning, or rather, that was the acknowledgement of the beginning. Almost every day after school, she would meet him. Occasionally they would risk a walk together, but usually they stayed indoors, because it was more in tune with a clandestine affair. They were deeply in love, though neither of them would risk talking of their future. John knew as well as Esther that a marriage between them was impossible. There were times when Esther refused to recognize its impossibility, and at these times, she would suggest breaking their relationship. Then they could avoid each other for two or three weeks, but inevitably they would come together again.

Their friendship continued for almost two years before David looked at her that day in the synagogue. She responded with affection, but primarily with gratitude, because she saw in David a way of extricating herself from a relationship which she knew could end only in unhappiness. So she saw less of John, and tried desperately to respond to David's love. But she had to admit to herself that it was impossible. Nevertheless, she decided to marry David; she thought that the legality of their partnership might in time, free her. But her deception of them both agonized her, and desperate to unburden herself of her dilemma, she told Norman she wanted to talk to him. Her parents would never have listened to her, and Bella wouldn't have understood, so it was Norman she chose, because though she liked him little, she respected his intelligence and understanding.

They were alone in the flat together, and she came straight to the point. 'I'm not in love with David,' she said.

She thought he smiled, and she attributed it to his nervousness at their unaccustomed intimacy. 'I'll never love him,' she added.

'Then why are you going to marry him?'

'I've got to,' she said. 'It's the only way I can break the other thing.'

'John?' he said.

'How did you know?'

'I guessed. About two years?' he said, rather smugly, Esther thought. 'Don't worry,' he added. 'No one else has the slightest suspicion.'

'But how did you find out?'

'Well, I see quite a lot of John at the library. He's never told me, but I can tell by the way he talks about you. Anyway,' he laughed, 'you're made for each other, you two. Why don't you just accept it.'

She was enormously grateful to him for his understanding to the point of sanctioning their affair. 'But I can't marry him,' she said.

'Why not?'

She was horrified at his callousness. 'But I can't do that to Mom and Pop. Mom maybe, but not to Pop. It would break him.'

'Parents don't break that easily,' he said. 'They'll get hysterical, and they'll get over it. If you love each other, this is what you must do.'

'I can't,' she said. 'They'd never forgive me. In any case, what would happen to David? What would he feel?'

Norman leaned forward. 'D'you really want to know?' he said. 'D'you really want to know what David would feel if you didn't marry him?'

She was surprised at the obvious significance he was giving her question. 'Yes,' she said, unsure. 'I want to know how he would feel.'

'Relieved,' he said. 'Utterly and absolutely relieved.'

She stared at him, incredulous.

'Look,' he said, 'I wouldn't tell you this unless you needed to know, and it's obvious that you do, and right now. I thought you might have found it out for yourself. But David, you see,' he spoke slowly now to give his words more emphasis, 'David is intending to marry you for exactly the same reason as you intend to marry him. He too, wants to break a habit.'

'Is there someone else?' she said. She felt a slight twinge of jealousy. 'But then,' she added, 'then we could help each other. We can be honest with each other from the start.'

'Well,' Norman began, 'it's not as simple as all that. His habit is not quite the same as yours.'

'What is it then?' she was irritated by her own lack of perception.

'Haven't you guessed?' he said. 'You've known him long enough.'

She couldn't imagine what there was in David's habit that was so strange and complicated. 'No, I haven't guessed,' she said. 'You'd better tell me.'

'Well,' he said, 'this might shock you. But he doesn't have other women.' He looked at her for some glimmer of understanding, but she stared at him, bewildered still. 'He . . . he likes men, Esther,' he said. 'He's basically a homosexual.'

It was a word that she'd often read in books, and she knew its meaning. But she had relegated the word to ancient history or other lands, because she could not envisage that it could have anything to do with her or her environment. Her first reaction was one of sour distaste, and anger that she had been so deceived, but then she felt pity for him, and abundant relief that Norman had told her in time. 'Then of course, I can't marry him,' she said. 'That's completely out of the question.'

Norman smiled again, and she couldn't understand why it was a smiling matter. 'Why are you smiling?' she said.

'I'm not smiling,' he said eagerly. 'I'm nervous. I'm relieved I suppose, that you know the truth. But you're right,' he said, 'and I'm glad it's your decision. You can't marry him. You must break it off.'

But she was not strong enough to make any decision. 'I can't,' she said. 'What could I tell him. He must never know that I know. And I can't tell Mom and Pop either. I couldn't bear their disappointment. They see me married already. They're already talking about their grandchildren.'

'Isn't it time we stopped doing things for their sake?' he said.

'Isn't it time we started doing things for ourselves? Look at Bella, chained to them for the rest of her life. Look at me. Twenty-six years old and still living at home. For their sake, 'cos they robbed me of the guts to be me. Listen Esther,' he said, 'if you can't face them in their disappointment, get out. Go, and say nothing beforehand. That's what I should have done. But I wanted discussion, I wanted blessings,' he laughed. 'You couldn't discuss it with them. They'd root you to the ground with guilt, and you'll end up like Bella. Go with John. Marry him, and be happy.'

'You're right,' she said. 'I haven't got the courage to face them. So I'll have to go. I'll leave them a letter,' she said appalled at her own weakness. 'But I won't marry John,' she said more firmly. 'I couldn't do that.'

'You must,' he said even more firmly. 'It's you who's marrying, Esther,' he said. 'Not them. If you don't want to marry immediately, you can wait. But tell them you're married. Let them think it's a *fait accompli*. Write it in the letter. I'll draft it for you.'

She was curious about his eagerness, and he sensed it. 'I don't want you to end up like Bella,' he explained. 'And one day, you'll be grateful.'

She insisted that she would not marry John, but he talked her into telling them that she had, otherwise, for what reason in their eyes, had she left home. 'Unless,' he added, 'you want to tell them about David, and that would hardly be fair to David or his mother.'

Now he had really trapped her. Staying at home was unthinkable. And so he had drafted the letters, one to their parents, and the other, with infinite care and love, to David.

And so it was arranged. While Esther made her preparations, she questioned her brother's motives. His eagerness to push her into marriage with John, puzzled her, and she could find no answer for it. She had been moved by his own admission of failure regarding his own freedom, which would give him added cause to wish for hers. She had no intention of marrying John. She was leaving home, because it was easier than staying, because she could not bear the blame for her parents' disappointment. She was grateful to Norman who had been able to define her weakness as strength.

As for Norman, he felt little scruple for what he had done. He talked himself into believing that David had a problem and that marriage would be no solution. He was doing him a favour. He wanted David for himself, and his need for him made it right and proper.

And so the letter had been found, and afterwards, David's body. She was alone in John's flat when Norman came to tell her. He lurched through the doorway, drunk with weeping, and fell into a chair, his head in his hands.

'Is Mom all right?' she whispered. His sobbing was uncontrollable. 'Is Pop all right?' She was terrified at the thought of the news he had brought, and instinctively she blamed him for whatever had happened. 'What have you come for?' she screamed at him.

He looked up without seeing her. 'It's David,' he said. 'You killed him.'

She did not immediately take in the second piece of information, but she heard it, and she stored it to deal with later. 'Did he have an accident?' she said. She refused to equate David's death with her letter.

'He did it himself,' Norman said quietly. '*You* go and tell his mother. He did it when he read your letter.'

'*My* letter?' she whispered. 'It was *your* letter,' she pleaded. She had to sort that out first. The grief would keep for later, and she knew bitterly how well it would keep. 'It was your letter,' she said again.

'He's dead,' he wept. 'Why did you have to do it?'

'Relief, you said. Utter and complete relief, you said, when I asked you how David would feel. That's what you told me.' She took him by the shoulders and shook him with her hatred. 'You *knew* he loved me, didn't you.'

'Come home, Esther,' he said broken, 'you've got to come home.'

She took her hands off him, stupefied by his request. 'Oh no,' she said, and she was astonished at the aged bitterness in her voice, 'oh no, you caused it, and you're going to pay for it. You bought my guilt, and you can take it home, and you can live with it for the rest of your life. And together with your little lot,' she said bitterly, 'it'll make a fine parcel. Take it home, yours and mine, and I hope it will rot you.' She hated herself for her glib and ready cruelty, and when he had gone, she gave way to her grief and acknowledged her share of the blame. It seemed now almost incumbent on her to marry John, so that David's death would not have been entirely without cause. But her love for John was slowly evaporated by her grief, and she punished herself into marriage. That too, Norman could carry with him. But a month later, when she went through the marriage ceremony, it was David she married, which was why she had shaved her head.

Rabbi Zweck took her hand. 'You stay a little here?' he said. 'You don't have to rush home?'

'This is home,' she said gently. 'I'm not going back. I'm staying with you and Bella.'

Auntie Sadie sighed. 'Just like the old days it'll be. You'll be better, Abie, and Norman will come home, and why not,' she said, 'a little happiness for us all.'

Nobody questioned Esther's decision, and she was grateful for it. 'Tomorrow we'll all go and see Norman,' she said. It would be her last hurdle home.

18

Nobody at the hospital had informed Norman's home of his latest breakdown. Had Bella telephoned, she would have been issued with the standard comuniqué that he was under sedation, which was their euphemism for his hooliganism and their inability to cope with it. Rabbi Zweck was excited at the prospect of a visit. It was over a month since he had seen Norman, and this time, he was bringing special visitors. It would be quite a family reunion and he had high hopes of it. Esther was nervous. She had no idea what she would say to him. She shrank from the neatness and uniformity of his confines, and she pitied him. She could make no preparation for their meeting. She would have to wait for his reactions to her, and they might well be hostile.

Rabbi Zweck led the way along the corridor, like a guide, nodding to some of the familiar faces. 'In the ward at the bottom,' he said, turning back to them. 'Come, let's go inside.' He stood aside to let them go through. 'Such a surprise he'll have. He wanted to wait by the door, as a spectator, to see Norman's reaction to Esther, and as he waited, the nurse on duty went over to him. 'Rabbi Zweck,' he said gently, 'could you come into my room a moment?'

Rabbi Zweck trembled and followed him. 'Is something the matter?' he said. His voice was timid, as if admitting some responsibility.

'Sit down,' McPherson said. 'It's nothing serious. It's just that yesterday we had a little trouble in the ward' – he did not want to mention Minister's death – 'and a number of patients were upset by it. Norman had a slight breakdown so we put him under sedation again. He was doing so well, it's a pity. It's a bit of a set-back for him. But there's no need to upset yourself. It's only temporary and he'll be on the mend again shortly.'

Rabbi Zweck's reaction was one of anger. 'He should be at home,' he said. 'He hasn't got enough trouble, he should be upset by other people. I take him home,' he said defiantly.

'That's impossible,' McPherson said. 'He's committed in any case for another three weeks. We would only have to bring him back.'

Rabbi Zweck shuddered at the recollection of his first journey to the hospital with Norman; he couldn't endure another. 'Can we sit with him?' he asked timidly. He was angry at his own abdication. So often since Norman's illness he had felt the same anger when he had been obliged to bow to an authority he did not trust, because his own ignorance made him powerless.

He felt a slight twinge in his arm, the old familiar pain. But he was not afraid. His weapon was his love which he was now turning in on himself.

'Go and sit by his bed,' McPherson said. 'You can talk to him a little, but you'll find him very drowsy.'

Rabbi Zweck went into Norman's ward. Bella was sitting at the bottom of the bed, and Auntie Sadie was peering into his face. She had come to see him, and see him she would. Esther stood on one side. She had been dreading the meeting, and now she was half relieved, that it was postponed. She could gradually get used to him, until perhaps there would be no need for words at all. He looked very young while he slept, she thought, and innocent of all the hurt he had done them. She saw that his hair had thinned, but his face in repose was unlined and peaceful. She was curious about his body and though she never remembered seeing it, even as a young child, its contours suddenly became important to her. She needed to see it to confirm the years that had parted them, for a moment she had lost all sense of their separation. She brought a chair for her father as he came over, and she stood apart from them, staring at Norman's inert body, and inwardly she wept for what they had all been reduced to.

Rabbi Zweck leaned over the bed, and touched Norman's shoulder. 'Norman,' he said, 'is Poppa. Poppa's come to see you. Who says I'm ill? I'm here by your bed. Is Poppa, Norman. Say hullo to your Poppa.' He shook him slightly, and

Auntie Sadie tried to stay his hand. None of them could bear to look at his face. 'Poppa is here,' he said again. 'So well I am. You shouldn't worry I was ill. You hear me, Norman?'

'He knows you're here,' Bella said. 'Don't aggravate yourself.'

'Norman,' he tried again, but Esther pulled him back gently into his chair. 'Rest Poppa,' she said, then looking at the others, 'I don't see any point in this.' She was suddenly irritated by their despair. Norman lay there motionless and withdrawn, yet his power over the figures around him was irrefutable, and she wanted to beat him into consciousness and show him what he had done. 'How d'you stand it, Bella?' she said. 'How can you be so calm?'

'I've had lots of rehearsals,' she said. 'You get used to it after a time.' She smiled at her sister. Already she felt the relief of sharing the burden and suddenly it seemed not a burden at all.

Rabbi Zweck turned away from the bed, and as he did so, he saw a familiar face sitting up in the bed alongside. He was staring across the ward with a look that reminded Rabbi Zweck of his first visit to the hospital. He looked at the bed opposite and it was empty. That's where the stare had first come from, that insolent upright face opposite Norman's bed. He did not know why, but he shivered at its absence. It had become a familiar sight in the ward, and he was frightened by the disappearance of a known and recognized feature of Norman's new abode. He had left the same fear when, one day, Billy was no longer there. Now this man, staring in the bed alongside Norman, was vainly trying to keep up the old appearance of the ward, but he wore the look like an ill-fitting inheritance. 'Where's Minister?' Rabbi Zweck shouted, suddenly recalling the name of the absentee. A few patients in the ward turned to look at him, and as Rabbi Zweck stared back, he noticed that not one single face was familiar, that everything in fact had changed in the ward, but for his heap of son lying in sad and stubborn permanence.

He remembered the familiarity of the face sitting up in the bed, and he turned round, desperate to communicate with it, to find some common ground that it might share with Norman.

The face smiled at him, and the smile too was familiar, an unaimed affable affair, that flickered on and off like a dying lamp. It was Billy and Rabbi Zweck was overjoyed to see him. Not all of them had gone and left his sleeping son. Billy was there holding the fort and he would leave the ward only when Norman was ready to go. 'William?' he said. 'You remember me? It's a long time I haven't seen you. Are you better?'

'I came back this morning?' Billy smiled. 'Yes, I'm better.'

'Is your mother coming today?' Rabbi Zweck hoped so. They too could lend familiarity to the place. They too would stay until all could leave together. 'So glad I am to see you,' Rabbi Zweck said. He went close to the bed. 'William,' he whispered, 'what happened to Minister?'

'He's dead,' he said. 'Yesterday he did himself in. Pity.'

Rabbi Zweck shivered. He thought of Minister's parents, if he had any, and pitied them, and he was angry with himself that he had disliked him. But at the same time, he found himself cursing Minister for having shocked his own son into a deep sleep. He tried in his own sorrow to weep for others but he couldn't, and he was ashamed of his loss of compassion. But William was real and alive, though god knows what rot his mind had reaped from his years of sojourn in this place. 'When he wakes up, my son,' he said to himself, 'I take him home. No matter what. We take him home.'

He went back to Norman's bed. Auntie Sadie was stroking Norman's forehead. Occasionally he stirred and groaned. Bella rested her hand on the lopsided tent his legs had made, and Esther stood apart, sickened by it all. 'I don't see the point in staying,' she suddenly said.

'Sit a minute, Esther,' her father said. He was loath to leave Norman. He harboured vague hopes that Norman would wake, just long enough to see him there, and to know that he was not ill. Yet he knew that he was ill. He had felt progressively worse since coming there, and the news of Minister's death had stabbed him with yet another pain. 'I am close, I am close,' he muttered to himself. He wanted to stay by Norman, not for Norman's sake, but for his own, for he felt that soon enough, they would be parted for ever. 'Sit a little, Esther,' he said, patting the end of the bed.

She came and sat near him. There was nothing they could say to each other, transfixed as they were by the sleeping figure, afraid to interrupt his silent prone power.

'Is good he's sleeping,' Auntie Sadie whispered. 'We'll sit a little, and we'll go home and make a nice lemon tea. Then we make arrangements he should come home. His Auntie Sadie should look after him. Won't she, Norman,' she said, stroking his forehead once more. 'Such a baby he looks.' Yes, they were all babies, Rabbi Zweck thought. He looked at his two daughters, and saw them innocent and dependent as children, and he knew again that he was leaving them, and all he could bequeath was the heap on the bed. 'Norman, wake up,' he whispered desperately, 'wake up before I go.'

Norman turned fitfully in his sleep, and Rabbi Zweck leaned forward in his chair. But Norman settled again, his head upright on the pillow, his chin thrust forward proudly. His look of tranquillity willed them to stay by his side. So they sat there, on guard and watched him in silence.

A black shadow was beating on Norman's brow, and he wished to god it would go away. He tried to call out but his mouth was stiff and dry. He tried to raise his hands to wipe it away, but they had melted inseverable into his sides. He lay there helpless while the beating black shadow filtered into his brain, and the hammering began. He wondered how such nebulous stuff as shadow could beat with such precise and insistent rhythm, and how it could make any impression on the stuff his brain was made of. And so he concluded that his brain had turned to foam. He tried again to beat his hand on his brow, but he had to acknowledge that he had lost sway over his body, that it was now in other hands.

The foam swelled to the opposite wall of the ward, and there were several shadows in the swell, and he smiled to see that they were drowning. For a moment the hammering stopped, until a black shadow stained the foam with the promise of a glass of lemon tea. His hands were free again, and he drowned her because her solicitude was familiar and painful. The foam swelled back to his own wall, and the shadows broke on his mind like flotsam. There was one that Norman desperately wanted to save, but he couldn't without saving them all. But he only wanted that one, that one dark shadow that sunk lower than all the rest, that weak one, that good one that he needed so desperately to keep alive, just long enough for the terrible tide to ebb. So he saved them all, and the small shadow swelled with gratitude. 'Don't aggravate,' he heard. That was his mother with her aggravation, but he couldn't find her shadow anywhere. He was worried that he had overlooked it in the general wreckage of his mind. He felt it pinning him down like an anchor, but he could find no trace of it. The hammering started again, and again his hands clung to him. He forced a swelling of the foam again, and this time it got bigger and bigger, until he realized with sickening gloom, that once more it was beyond his control. He watched it swell to the limits of the walls of the ward, hammering at his skull in its spreading. He waited for it to reach its peak, because he knew that then the pain would subside, but the tide withdrew before its fulfilment, like a wave that changes its mind about breaking, like an orgasm that thwarts itself, and the swell shrank, but the pain was no less. But as it neared him again, back to his own self and his own wall, it took on a greater swelling. Break, break, for god's sake, he tried to call out. 'I am closer, closer,' he heard his father say, and he feared the tide would overwhelm them all. Then suddenly it broke on the jagged corners of his mind, and he felt no pain. All the shadows had gone, and the hammering had stopped. He felt the gentle foam rippling into his eyes and he saw that it had turned to red. His eyes were bleeding tears, and the silver-fish slithered into the dryness of his throat where they struggled and died. And then the hammering started again and the foam burst the opposite wall. He had to keep away from the swell, so he shrank from it, smaller and smaller, until he was a tiny pinpoint separate on a raft, and he looked across at the wreckage with the elation of a survivor. Then a shadow loomed at his side. 'I don't see the point in staying,' he heard. 'Go, go,' Norman tried to call, and he pushed it overboard. He wanted to get back into the swell again. It was safer there, steeped in his own self-built havoc, and he fought his way into the foam as it swelled from wall to wall. He struggled to the surface, lifting his head high, and with his chin thrust forward, the shadows were invisible.

Rabbi Zweck looked at his son's face and he was satisfied that he knew he was there. He saw Billy's parents come in through the door and he felt an immediate warmth towards them. They too were glad to be back in familiar surroundings. Over the past month, their visits with Billy had been silent too, but surrounded by more blatant lunacy than here. They looked at the heap of Norman on the bed, and silently transmitted their sympathy. 'Not well again?' Billy's mother said.

'Is all right,' Rabbi Zweck answered quickly. 'Just asleep he is. A couple weeks he sleeps, then is everything all right.' He was sickened by his own optimisim. 'Your son is back, I see.'

'Yes,' his mother said. 'He had a nasty turn. But we're all right now, aren't we,' she said, patting Billy on the head. 'Back to work next week, aren't we,' she said, 'with your poor mother running short of stock for her bazaar.'

Billy smiled in her direction, and shook hands with his father. Rabbi Zweck was moved by the formality of the gesture. It gave back to each of them the dignity that the mother was forever trying to snatch away.

Rabbi Zweck introduced his family. He remembered the initial hostility he'd felt for these two people, and he bitterly regretted his contempt. So now he wanted to make amends, and what better way than by donating his family to them. He settled them around Billy's bed, where they were all grateful for the conversation and activity, and then he returned to Norman and sat there and watched. He felt for Norman's hand underneath the sheet and he held it in his own. As he gripped it, he felt a definite response, and his heart filled with overwhelming joy. 'Is Poppa, Norman,' he whispered. 'Together we are.' He squeezed his son's hand, and again the same response and he thought his joy would break him. Then he felt a stab of pain in his back, and he fell forward on to the bed, groaning.

Bella rushed to her father's side, while Auntie Sadie, summoning up the situation in one glance, ran outside the ward to fetch help. Esther remained at Billy's bedside, unable to move. Auntie Sadie returned with McPherson and two men carrying a stretcher. Gently they gathered him up and laid him down, still groaning a little, though the pain had eased. Then they carried him towards the door of the ward. Auntie Sadie walked alongside, and Bella followed. 'Come,' she said, turning to Esther, her hand outstretched. She was suddenly sorry for her. She had missed out on the living, if you could call it that; the twin harvests of her forgiveness lay inert and incommunicable. She took Bella's hand, like a novice.

As they neared the door, Rabbi Zweck gesticulated with his hands, and the stretcher-bearers stopped, while McPherson bent his ear to hear what Rabbi Zweck was trying to say. Then whether he had heard it or not, with supreme understanding, he ordered the bearers to turn the stretcher around, so that Rabbi Zweck could see his son for the last time. Bella and Esther held their father's hands, while he stared fixedly at everything in the world that he would bequeath them. It was all that he had to live for, and he loved it now with a love that was killing him.

19

They took him to a small private room at the end of the corridor. They laid him on the bed, watching and waiting until the doctor arrived. He wanted to speak to them and they tried to quieten him.

'Save your strength,' Auntie Sadie said.

'For what?' they heard him say. Then, 'Thank you,' he murmured, trying to locate McPherson among the figures around his bed.

'When's the doctor coming,' Esther said, unwilling to acknowledge the natural consequences of the situation. She saw how Bella had already accepted it, holding her father's hand as she would do until the end. They saw him smile suddenly, and Auntie Sadie stroked his forehead. 'Such a place I should die in,' he murmured. 'Who is *meshugga*, after all?'

They tried to silence him, but he would have his say. He gestured to them to come close, and they each held some part of him, pumping his hands and shoulders as if to inject their own lives into him. 'Bella,' he whispered, 'Esther, Sadie, come. Say with me the *Shema*.' Bella had already accepted her father's death with a calculated storing of her grief. And for Auntie Sadie, this kind of scene almost inevitably marked the termination of her employment. So neither of them shrank from Rabbi Zweck's request. It was Esther who refused to comply.

'Poppa,' she said, 'there's no need. You will live. Don't give in. You'll get over it, like the last attack.'

'Is like Norman,' he said quietly. 'Norman also will get over it, and then again it starts. Often enough I have been dying. I'm tired already. Please say with me the *Shema*. Bellale, you begin.'

It was a reversal of the roles they had played all their lives, when he had been their teacher and had led them. Now he was asking Bella to lead him. It was his way of appointing her as his heir, for who after all was the head of the family, if not the one who led them in prayer.

'*Shema*,' Bella said softly.

Rabbi Zweck repeated it after her, and Sadie joined in.

'No, please no,' Esther tried to interrupt.

'Say it, Esther,' Rabbi Zweck said. 'You'll feel better.'

The words dried on her lips, but she managed to mouth the final abdication. '*Shema Yisroel*,' he said, and his voice became stronger, leading as of old, the chorus of his flock, '*adonai elohanu, adonai echod*.'

'Hear O Irael,' Auntie Sadie said, possibly for the benefit of McPherson, who stood at the foot of the bed, sad and bewildered. 'Hear O Israel, the Lord thy God, the Lord is One.'

And McPherson repeated it after her. He too wanted to abide by Rabbi Zweck's passing.

None of them noticed the doctor come in. His visit had by now become an irrelevancy. They watched him dispassionately as he came over to the bed. They withdrew their hands that held him, and made room for the cold instrument he placed on their father's chest.

'Let it be, let it be,' Rabbi Zweck muttered. 'It has heard my *Shema*. It agrees.' A faint smile crossed his face. 'And thank you,' he added.

The doctor took the stethescope away. He looked at Bella, the only one outside Rabbi Zweck's line of vision, and he shook his head. She nodded and thanked him. He took McPherson to the door, spoke to him in whispers, then he left without looking behind him.

The three women approached the bed again and held him. 'I sleep now,' he said. He sensed the acute melancholy gathered around him. 'I sleep a little,' he amended. He rested his head sideways on the pillow and closed his eyes.

They heard him muttering, and Bella bent close. 'Sarah,' she heard, and the name was repeated. And then, rather hoarsely, 'Norman, forgive me,' he said. 'Forgive. Is all my fault.' He opened his eyes again and he saw what he was leaving. Two sad unmarried daughters, one with her earnest *scheitel*, and in another room, his broken son. 'I failed,' he muttered. 'Forgive.'

He closed his eyes again, and they knew it was now only a matter of waiting. But they held his hands still, until they could be sure that he was alone.

McPherson left the room, not so much out of respect for their privacy, but because, had he stayed, the sobs that were shaking him, could have broken and disturbed their serenity. He had met Rabbi Zweck only a few times during his visits, but he had been infinitely moved by his bewilderment, his childish optimism, his unswerving faith. Now he was dying, and though it was a fearless death, it was not a peaceful one. Rabbi Zweck knew well the chaos he was leaving behind, and he blamed himself for it.

Inside the room, they waited. It had been a long afternoon of watching and waiting. At Norman's bedside, every movement of his face, the slightest twitch of his body was noted and responded to. Here, the body was still, undisturbed by the light irregular breathing. They counted each breath as he exhaled and waited trembling for the next. Each in their own minds gave him a certain number of breaths more, and if he could conquer that number, then he could survive.

Esther began to weep, and Bella comforted her, as she had done with Norman when her mother had died. It was her strength to comfort and sustain, and she had a fleeting feeling that she would have to survive them all.

They stood by his side for a long time. Occasionally they stroked his forehead. There was a slight pulse in his temple and it was cool. Bella held her fingers close, as if to encourage its beating. Auntie Sadie shook her head with the weariness of one who had seen it so often before.

The door opened, and when they looked around, it seemed that it had opened of its own accord, since no one was standing on the threshold. It seemed to them all that the Angel of Death was calling it a day. They looked quickly at Rabbi Zweck, but he was still breathing gently. Then at the door again, and Billy, with his dressing-gown wound loosely about him, stepped timidly towards the bed. He looked at Rabbi Zweck, and then at the women. 'I'm sorry,' he said. 'I liked him a lot. He called me William.' Then he knelt at the foot of the bed, and prayed. He prayed silently for a long time. The women didn't look at him. On the one hand, they were moved by his gesture, but on the other they felt a certain distaste that their father should be dispatched by a lunatic's prayer. When he had finished, he looked again at the sleeping form. 'Thank you,' he said, and he left the room.

As soon as he had gone, Bella and the others recited the *Shema* again, loud and clear to sweep away any possible blasphemy that Billy had left at the foot of the bed, And so, amply fortified by both God and His Son, Rabbi Zweck died, and they took away their hands.

In the ward at the end of the corridor, Norman stirred violently in his sleep. He awoke with a start, but finding no one at his side who could have awakened him, he took it for a bad dream, and he sighed back into his sleep.

20

They let Norman's deep sleep run its course. And when they woke him, they eased him for a few days back to his normal routine. And then they told him.

Norman came back to the ward from the nurse's room. The feeling of remorse and repentance that was the aftermath of his sedation in no way helped to cushion the shattering news of his father's death. He had received it better had he been violent. But in his present state, anxious to atone, eager to be forgiven, there was now no point in either. It was too late for contrition. His time-honoured status as scapegoat was one that at last he himself would gladly assume, and there was a little peace in that. He buried his face in his hands. In the nurse's room outside he had listened attentively while the doctor had had his say. He had asked no questions; he had simply stood there, collecting a series of words, and now he was alone and he had to assemble them.

But when this was done, and he could say to himself, 'My father is dead,' and a little later, 'Poppa is dead,' still something impeded his full-hearted weeping. He tried to understand why the tears would not flow. Perhaps it was the location of his father's death that blocked them, the sense of degradation he must have felt, the utter humiliation that he could not keep it in until he'd reached his own bed. It was his fault, Norman admitted to himself, the site of his father's passing, and even perhaps, the death itself. Desperately he recalled the moments of pleasure he had given his father during his life-time, to offset this terrible feeling of guilt. He was grateful for each single recollection, but his eyes remained dry, though his grief was choking him. He pictured his father lying in the ward, only a few yards away from where he now was sitting. He had slept through his dying, his death, his funeral and the mourning. He had slept through it all. And now he was experiencing each event in its turn. He had to experience them; it was his right as a son. He saw his father's coffin lowered and he saw himself indifferently asleep. He saw Bella sitting on a low stool, and he heard the men's nightly prayers, but he, the eldest son, was still sleeping. And still the tears did not come.

He felt a hand on his shoulder. He looked up and saw Billy, smiling his aimless smile. 'I saw him,' Billy said. 'He died in peace. I prayed for him. I asked Jesus to take him to heaven.'

Norman shook his hand off his shoulder. He clenched his teeth and trembled with loathing. What right had this madman to see his father off? What right had he to pray for him. And to Jesus, for Christ's sake, that word that for close on seventy years had stuck in his father's throat.

Billy stood there bewildered. 'I went for you, Norman,' he said timidly. 'You were sleeping, so I went on your behalf.'

Norman touched his arm. He regretted his ingratitude. He wanted so desperately to pray. He felt that if he could pray, the tears would come. But how could he say *Kaddish* for his father, if his heart were not in the prayer. How long ago, Norman thought, had he truly believed, and when and at what precise moment, had he lost his faith. He thought back to his adolescence and he realized that it had come upon him slowly, sparked off by his father's deep-rooted belief that the Jews were the chosen people. He had never been able to accept that, and he refused to accept it now, even though it meant that he could pray, and he cursed the Jewish God for having paralysed his tongue.

A hot anger simmered inside him and he stood up by his bed. 'Dear God,' he shouted, then 'Dearest God,' overlaying his affection to offset his own fury. 'Why did You choose us? Are we Your family, and did You choose us as Your scapegoat for all Your neuroses? Did You elect us to carry Your wrath, Your jealousy, Your expectation, Your omnipotence, Your mercy and pity, Your sheer bloody-mindedness?' He sat on the bed trembling. He looked at Billy and realized the futility of his cursing. He and Billy were neighbours in a lunatic asylum, and no single word could divide them. They were both past God, past Jesus, past anybody's pickings, for they were the chosen ones, and they answered only to themselves.

Yet why were they all there? Why were *they* the élite and no other? And he began to examine himself with the cold logic of his saner years. He thought of his family, because it was they, he had to admit, who had put him there, when the burden they had loaded on him had become too heavy to bear. 'Bella can't grow up,' he said to himself, 'and I carry it. Esther married out, and I carry it. My father, God rest his soul, failed, and I carry it. My mother wouldn't let go, and finally broke my back. Together, they sucked the life out of me with ravenous appetite. Who am I, save their receptacle? Who am I save their "happenings"? Who am I save my own sad packaging?' He looked up at Billy pleadingly. 'Teach me how to pray.'

Billy took his hand. 'Come,' he said, 'we'll kneel down together.' But Norman shrank from that kind of idolatry. Kneeling was as blasphemous as the word Jesus, and he owed it to his father to deny those words as he had done. Confusion tore through him. All that was Jewish about him surged with a painful re-awakening. But Billy was by his side, and Billy had another god, and so did all those who surrounded him, the sad one in the corner, who had hugged the same corner for so long, the compulsive hand-washer forever at the sink at his rites, and the man who hummed and never spoke. He saw them all, and in them all, he saw his own loneliness and despair. He felt tears behind his eyes, and in that moment, he understood that his father had left him, that he was alone, that he could cry only for himself, and those around him. And the tears flooded the blockage, and he wept like a child bereaved.

He let go of Billy's hand. He had to pray on his own. He had to pray out of his own confusion, out of his own inherited permissible words. He would try. He put his hands together, and was pleased that the gesture, so long untried, had happened so naturally. He closed his eyes, and begged the old and ragged faith to enter him. '*Shema*,' he began. He started in Hebrew to clarify which god he was addressing, but he was conscious of Billy at his side and he had to pray for him too. 'Jesus,' he whispered. He momentarily checked on his addressee. He was glad that what they called his madness, had managed to transcend the childish obscenity of that word. 'Jesus,' he said, and moreover, 'sweet Jesus.' His sobs were choking him, not only for his father, whose peace he almost envied, but for himself, and Billy, and all those around him, so loosely tacked on to life. He looked around the ward and smelled its desolation. For loneliness smells, like a house of mourning smells. He looked at Billy, then at the chess-player, the swallower, the hand-washer and the hummer, and the tight-lipped sad in the corner. He remembered Minister too, and he gathered them all into his prayer. 'You,' he screamed to the ceiling, 'and you bloody well know who I mean.' He sank weeping on to his bed. 'Dear God,' he said. It was a word after all, that covered everybody. 'Look after us cold and chosen ones.'

Special Effects

BY HARRIET FRANK

Ever had the feeling that just about everything is collapsing
around you? Well that's the starting-point for Harriet Frank's
remarkable new novel *Special Effects*, the story of a
very special lady. Her name is Emma, and things – and come
to that, people! – have a habit of collapsing around her.
But Emma's speciality is survival, and this story of how she
faces up to everything that life can throw at her – with the
help of her own specially effective blend of panache and
earthy common sense – makes riveting and thoroughly
entertaining reading. If you enjoy the very best of
contemporary women's fiction, you'll be knocked out by
Harriet Frank's *Special Effects*, it's the kind of novel that will
leave no reader unaffected.

GENERAL FICTION   0 7221 3652 8   £1.25

and don't miss
SINGLE
also by Harriet Frank in Sphere Books

A selection of bestsellers from SPHERE

FICTION

BY REASON OF INSANITY	Shane Stevens	£1.75 ☐
THE ELECT	Gerald Suster	£1.25 ☐
SPECIAL EFFECTS	Harriet Frank	£1.25 ☐
BETHANY'S SIN	Robert R. McCammon	£1.40 ☐
NOW, GOD BE THANKED	John Masters	£1.95 ☐
SUMMER'S END	Danielle Steel	£1.25 ☐

FILM AND TV TIE-INS

THE EMPIRE STRIKES BACK	Donald F. Glut	£1.00 ☐
FAME	Leonore Fleischer	£1.25 ☐
NIJINSKY	Romola Nijinsky	£1.50 ☐
MIDNIGHT EXPRESS	Billy Hayes	£1.00 ☐

NON-FICTION

NAZI GOLD	Ian K. Sayer and H. L. Seaman with Frederick Nolan	£1.50 ☐
A NURSE'S WAR	Brenda McBryde	£1.25 ☐
A VIEW FROM A BROAD	Bette Midler	£4.95 ☐
TIMEWARPS	John Gribbin	£1.25 ☐
TRUE BRITT	Britt Ekland	£1.25 ☐
PUT TO THE TEST	Geoff Boycott	£1.25 ☐

All Sphere books are available at your local bookshop or newsagent, or can be ordered direct from the publisher. Just tick the titles you want and fill in the form below.

Name _____

Address _____

_____

Write to Sphere Books, Cash Sales Department, PO Box 11, Falmouth, Cornwall TR10 9EN

Please enclose cheque or postal order to the value of the cover price plus:

UK: 30p for the first book, 15p for the second and 12p per copy for each additional book ordered to a maximum charge of £1.29

OVERSEAS: 50p for the first book and 15p for each additional book

BFPO & EIRE: 30p for the first book, 15p for the second book plus 12p per copy for the next 7 books, thereafter 6p per book.

Sphere Books reserve the right to show new retail prices on covers which may differ from those previously advertised in the text or elsewhere, and to increase postal rates in accordance with the PO.